Lessons from the Nahjul Balagha

Ayatullah Sayyid Ali Khamenei

Copyright

Copyright © 2021 al-Burāq Publications.

All rights reserved. No part of this publication may be reproduced, distributed, or transmitted in any form or by any means, including photocopying, recording, or other electronic or mechanical methods, without the prior written permission of the publisher, except in the case of brief quotations embodied in critical reviews and certain other noncommercial uses permitted by copyright law. For permission requests, write to the publisher, addressed "Attention: Permissions [Lessons from the Nahjul Balagha]," at the email address below.

ISBN: 978-1-956276-07-7.

Printed and published by al-Burāq Publications.

Ordering Information

We offer discounts and promotions for wholesale purchases and for non-profit organizations, libraries, and other educational institutions. Contact us at the email below for further information.

www.al-Buraq.org

publications@al-Buraq.org

First printed edition | October 2021

Dedication

The publication of this book was made possible through the generous support of our donors.

Please recite *Sūrah al-Fātiha* and ask Allāh for the Divine reward (*thawāb*) to be conferred upon the donors and the souls of all the deceased in whose memory their loved ones have contributed graciously towards the publication of *Lessons from the Nahjul Balagha*.

Duaa al-Hujja

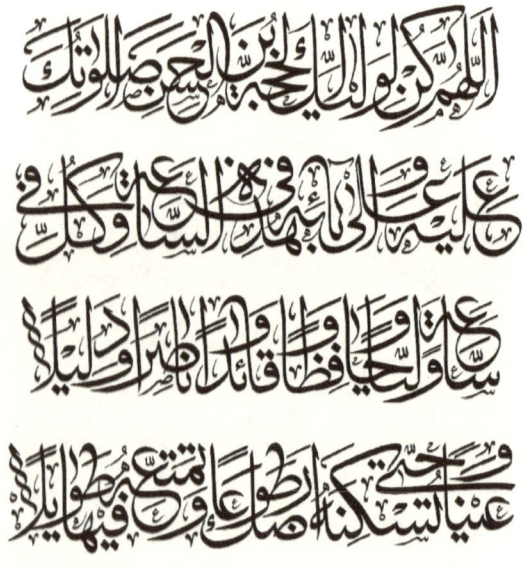

O Allah, be, for Your representative, the Hujjat (proof), son of al-Hasan, Your blessings be upon him and his forefathers, in this hour and in every hour: a guardian, a protector, a leader, a helper, a proof, and an eye - until You make him live on the Earth, in obedience (to You), and cause him to live in it for a long time.

Table of Contents

Introduction 1

Introduction by the Translator 3

Introduction by the Author..7

    Fundamental Beliefs..24

    Social and Political Matters...25

    Morality 25

Lesson One: Prophethood (Nubuwwah)...................27

    Questions and Answers 42

Lesson Two: Background to Prophethood 47

    The Age of Ignorance..47

    Material Inadequacy..47

    Spiritual Inadequacy 48

    Questions and Answers 67

Lesson Three: To Which Class Of Society do The Prophets Belong?..73

    The Definition of the Deprived (mustad'af).............77

    Summary...87

    Questions and Answers 92

Lesson Four: How are Prophets Chosen?................97

    Summary...106

Lesson Five: Duties and Responsibilities of the
 Prophets...109
Lesson Six: The Continuity of Prophethood.........127
 Questions and Answers..141
Lesson Seven: The End of Prophethood.................145
 Questions and Answers..152
Lesson Eight: The Believer' Status Before, After and
 at the Time of the Prophets' Appearance 159
 The Three-Act Play of People's Status......................166
 Conclusion: Two General Points in the Sermon 169

Introduction

On the eve of 5th victorious anniversary of the glorious Islamic Revolution of Iran, and having gone through five years of struggles and achievements, we are witnessing great triumphs over all the colonizing plots of both eastern and western Superpowers and their mercenary agents, and are celebrating the Ten Days Dawn in a most splendid manner. The revolutionary Moslem people of Iran have triumphantly smashed down all the obstacles and bore all the problems imposed upon them by the criminal big powers, which wanted to weaken and break down the Islamic Revolution.

The revolutionary Islamic nation continues to resist like a firm mountain in spite of suffering the loss of so many martyrs in various scenes of combat imposed by stubborn murderous enemies of the Revolution.

The committed Iranian people steadfastly follow their reviving Islamic way-the way which has now become a model for all Moslems and oppressed nations and have created an Era of Spirituality that has severely terrified the arrogant world powers. This year, just as the preceding years, the Council for Ten Days Dawn Celebrations, on this auspicious occasion and for the purpose of presenting a lucid portrait of the Islamic Revolution and its Islamic and political lines, offers a number of books and pamphlets in various languages to the dear readers.

The present book-pamphlet is one of the said works and is offered to all whom it may interest and concern. We convey best wishes for the final victory of Islamic and Moslems in all arenas and forecast an ultimate defeat of the sinister international powers, while we pray for liberation of all oppressed and dominated peoples.

Council for Ten Days Dawn Celebrations

Introduction by the Translator

In the Name of Allāh, the Most Gracious, the Most Merciful

The book Lessons from the Nahjul Balaghah by the great Islamic scholar, Sayyid 'Ali Khamene'i, one of the leading theologians and politicians of Iran and presently its president and the Friday Ritual Prayer leader of Tehran, is a precious book presented to the world of Islam as a brief introduction to the vast phenomenon of prophethood as it appears in the Nahjul Balaghah of the Commander of the Faithful, 'Ali, peace be upon him.'

The efforts made in translating this book were aimed at providing the Muslims, and even non-Muslims, outside the country, who communicate in the English language, with a valuable interpretation of "Ali's sayings concerning the issue of prophethood. It is hoped that this aim has been achieved with this translation. Readers, however, are kindly asked to observe the following points:

1. The translator has adopted the method of "blank verse" in rendering the author's views into English. However, on many occasions, an exact, word-by-word translation has been employed.

2. In some rare cases, unnecessary or repeated parts of the original text have been omitted in translation.

3. The source for the translation of the Sermons of the Nahjul Balaghah has been Sayyid All Radis translation of it (1979, Tehran)

4. The Qur'anic verses have been taken from Marmaduke Pickthall's "The Glorious Koran".

April 1983, H. Vahid Dastjerdi

Introduction by the Author

In the Name of Allāh, the Most Gracious, the Most Merciful

It is necessary, at the beginning, to provide our brothers and sisters with a brief introduction to the Nahjul Balaghah. As you know, the Nahjul Balaghah is a collection of Sermons, Letters and miscellaneous Sayings left as a memorial from the Master of the Pious, the Commander of the Faithful, All, peace be upon him. This book is divided into three sections of Sermons, Letters and short Sayings or' wise Sayings' (hikam), as they are usually called, some of which have been selected from among the Sermons and Letters.

The Nahjul Balaghah dates back to about one thousand years ago when the late Sayyid Radi compiled these Letters and Sermons at the end of the third and the outset of the fifth century (400A.H.) the Hejra after. It is, thus, a one thousand year old book. It is to be noted, however, that before Sayyid Radi made efforts in compiling All's Sermons and Sayings, they were scattered in the books of the Traditions' and history. Other scholars had also begun to perform this task in one way or another, but no one succeeded in accomplishing what Sayyid Radi did. Therefore, we are indebted to the endeavors and initiatives of this great scholar who left the Nahjul Balaghah for us.

Another point to be noted here is that, in addition to the contents of the Nahjul Balaghah, a number of Sermons, Letters and short Sayings of 'Ali, peace be upon him, can be found in different books which recent scholars have tried to compile and introduce as appendices to the Nahjul Balaghah. Therefore, in addition to the Nahjul Balaghah, which is, in itself, a rich and invaluable treasure, here are some other books of All's Sayings which shall later be introduced to the readers in detail so that they may obtain a general acquaintance with

Introduction by the Author

the bibliography of the Nahjul Balaghah and its related books.

Another point to note about the Nahjul Balaghah concerns the invalidity of this book, a claim made by some people over the years. The motive behind such a claim can easily be surmised, that is, the subject matter of the Nahjul Balaghah threatened the interests of some groups or classes of people who therefore found the best device, to be discrediting the book itself. It is also true of the personality of individuals, and for this same reason those who considered the personality of Imam 'Ali Ibn Abi Talib, peace be upon him, to be against their personal or group interests, naturally tried to distort it. In the same manner, they claimed that the Nahjul Balaghah was invalid on the grounds that they said it was without any authority (sanad).

It is clear that the Nahjul Balaghah is in the category of Traditions upon which we depend for the understanding of Islamic teachings, as well as the Traditions of the Prophet and the Book (the Holy Qur'an).

There is no doubt as to the authority of the Holy Qur'an, but as to the Traditions, valid authorities are needed to remove any doubts, i.e., the narrators of a certain Tradition, including the Imams and the Prophet, should be known and trustworthy. This has always been the main concern of our great narrators and jurisprudents in eliciting and understanding the divine ordinances.

Thus, we have the 'science of rijal', which deals with the recognition of narrators of Traditions and the 'science of diraya' which concerns the recognition and analysis of Traditions and which determines the correct and the unreliable Traditions. Thus, this attention to detail that a Tradition must have an authority and that authority must be valid, is necessary. It is because of this that today great emphasis is put on expertise in understanding Islamic sciences. An individual, who is not an expert, accepts the Traditions, which accord with his own intellect, understanding and mental background and rejects all others. This leads to the weakening of the religion.

Introduction by the Author

When an expert wants to rely on a Tradition, he first tries to acknowledge its authority and validity through his special expertise. This necessity has been taken care of by our jurisprudents in their recognition and understanding of Islamic laws and regulations. Now, some people asserted that the Nahjul Balaghah, as a collection of Traditions, which should be based on valid authorities, was without any authority and, therefore, was invalid and unreliable.

As a matter of fact, in one way these people were telling the truth for no chain of narrators are mentioned in the Nahjul Balaghah in any of the Sermons so that they can be attributed to the Commander of the Faithful and the truthfulness of such narrators could be sought. However, in the books of Traditions such as Vasa-al-Shi'a, al-Kafi and the like, as well as in the old history books. such as those of Tabari, ibn Athir and Ya'qubi, no chain of authorities can be found concerning the contents of the Nahjul Balaghah.

Firstly, although the Nahjul Balaghah itself does not mention the chain of authorities and narrators, this can be checked in the Shi'ite and Sunni books of Traditions where from the Sermons, Letters and Sayings of this book have been extracted and compiled. Several years ago, one of the Arab writers wrote a book entitled Madarik Nahjul Balaghah wa Masanidu (The Documents and Authorities of Nahjul Balaghah) which may later be introduced to the readers in an analysis of the books written about the Nahjul Balaghah.

In this book, the writer has quoted the authentic authorities of the Sermons, Letters and Sayings of the Nahjul Balaghah from the books of the Traditions. it is therefore, concluded that the content, of the Nahjul Balaghah should not be considered to be without authority on the mere ground that the book itself does not mention any authority.

Secondly, although the authorities of Traditions are proper means of reliance or vice versa, the text of Traditions can also be a means of obtaining confidence for one who undertakes research, i.e. when you study a text and find its contents miraculous (as you will, God-Willing, observe when interpreting ''Ali's words), when you see that in one sentence the writer has referred to something beyond the prevailing mentality of his own time, which others have been able to understand only in the course of centuries, when you are faced with a saying that predicts future events which cannot be presaged except by the likes of Amir al-Muminin who are in contact with endless divine knowledge and, in addition to all these merits, when you observe the highly eloquent words and expressions of the writer, it becomes quite clear to you that he is not an ordinary human being and that his saying cannot be but those of an immaculate Imam.

Based upon this, Sayyid Radi states that certain words and expressions of the Nahjul Balaghah, are matchless in human expression, something which has never been opposed, in the course of one thousand years, by eloquent writers, Islamic thinkers and even the adversaries of Islam. These people have always accepted that some statements of the Nahjul Balaghah are superior to human expression and beyond the ordinary level of the human being's knowledge at that time. The conclusion is therefore drawn that, despite the absence of the chain of authorities and narrators in the Nahjul Balaghah, this book is undoubtedly that of the Commander of the Faithful and reliable as such.

Thirdly, as you know and as we mentioned previously, the Nahjul Balaghah consists of the Sermons (i.e. lectures, not the sermons delivered in the Friday ritual prayers, although the book may have included some of these sermons as well), Letters and short Sayings of 'Ali, peace be upon him, which he expressed and wrote as a teacher, ruler and an Islamologist. Thus, in addition to reflecting the general lines of Islamic thought, these Sermons and Letters also cover daily matters, i.e. the current problems and difficulties of Amir al Muminin's life.

In our own time, that is, after the victory of the Islamic Revolution, many similar aspects can be found between our social situation

Introduction by the Author

and that of Amir al-Muminin's time, although our situation is more similar in many respects (i.e. enemies, enmities and other problems) to the Medina social situation at the time of the Prophet's migration. The difference, however, between the social situation of ''Ali's rule and that of the Prophet lies in the fact that under the Prophet's rule, the enemy had a clear and well-known position, that is, not even one single group of the adversaries of Islam shared an aspect common to the Prophet.

The atheists among the Quraish, the Jews of Medina, the western and eastern superpowers of the time and the Christians of Najran, each had slogans of their own. In fact, there was no organized group to cry the same slogan as that of the Prophet and, at the same time, to stand openly against him in fight.

Accordingly, the Prophet suffered a great deal but never felt the heavy sorrows that 'Ali ibn Abi Talib tolerated during his reign.

There were hypocrites at the time of the Prophet as well but, first of all, they were not organized; secondly, they did not have a manifest position against the Prophet and they did not use the same slogans as those of the Prophet so that the people might doubt as to whether the Prophet was truthful or his rivals. Thirdly, the hypocrites were more or less known to all the people. For instance, everyone, including his own son, knew that Abdullah ibn Ubaid was the head of the hypocrites and even his son suggested to the Prophet to kill his father or prevent him from entering Medina if the Prophet permitted.

On the contrary, at the time of the rule of Amir al Muminin, those who fought him used exactly the same slogans as his. Moreover, they were among the distinguished personalities of the time, with long, past records. For example, the group of the Nakithin (the breakers of allegiance or the front in the 'Battle of the Camel' comprising Talha, Zubair and Ayesha) fought the Commander of the Faithful with his own slogans - slogans in favor of Islam and the truth.

Introduction by the Author

The group of Qasitin, (the front of Mu'awiya, the Damascus front), too, pretended in such a way that the impartial observers fell in a state of doubt as to which group was telling the truth. When you study Mu'awiya's letters to 'Ali, you find exactly the same words as those of 'Ali to him. For example, 'Ali addresses, "From the Commander of the Faithful, 'Ali ibn Abi Talib to Mu'awiya ibn Abi Sufyan", and Mu'awiya writes, "From the Commander of the Faithful, Mu'awiya ibn Abi Sufyan to All ibn Abi Talib".

Mu'awiya does not introduce himself as 'the commander of the faithless' or 'the commander of the polytheists' but, exactly like 'Ali, as the Commander of the Faithful. Then 'Ali advises Mu'awiya, for instance, to be pious to fear God and to refrain from wasting the blood of Muslims, and Mu'awiya uses the same advice for 'Ali.

Therefore, the problem of 'Ali is that his enemy is not a manifest enemy in the eyes of the people, for the enemy also offers whatever he offers and, as a result, he cannot show the real character of the opposing front to the people. It is true, of course, that 'Ali had a great deal to say but not all the words spoken can necessarily be understood by those who hear and this was ''Ali's constant sorrow.

Perhaps this was the reason why he used to sit beside a well and speak into it about his grievances. In fact, other than a group of people who were completely faithful to 'Ali for a special reason, and not because they observed his doings and prayers or they heard about Mu'awiya's evil deeds, others were always in doubt as to which side was telling the truth, for they witnessed, as an example, that in the Battle of Siffin, both sides performed the congregational ritual prayer with humility and modesty.

Thus, a hypocritical atmosphere was characteristic of society during the time of 'Ali. This does not imply, however, that all the people were hypocrites. Even the followers of Mu'awiya were a group of honest, tribal Arabs, from the area around Damascus, who had, from the very outset of

Introduction by the Author

their conversion to Islam, seen and known no governors except Mu'awiya and his family.[1]

They knew Islam through the words of these people. They had heard so many good things about them - that they were scribes of the divinely revealed Book, that since Mu'awiya's sister was the Prophet's wife and thus called 'Umm al-Mu'minin (mother of the believers), Mu'awiya was Khal al-Muminin (maternal uncle of the believers)[2] - that they supported Mu'awiya and fought against All with the best of intentions. So they were not hypocrites.

However, unlike the time of the Prophet, society enjoyed an air of hypocrisy, about which more explanation may, God-willing, be provided when discussing the words and sayings of the Commander of the Faithful.

---

[1] When Damascus was conquered by 'Umar, the second Caliph, he appointed Yazid bin Abu Sufyan the governor of that region and when Yazid died, his brother Mu'awiya took over. Thus, the people of the region came to know only Mu'awiya and his family from the very beginning when they embraced Islam.

[2] This title is still found in many books of our Sunni brethren.

This atmosphere of hypocrisy is also a peculiarity of our own time, although from the point of view of social conditions, enmities, manner of opposition, hostile parties and so forth, our time is more comparable to the time of the Prophet. Today, the so-called followers of 'progressive Islam' in our society are those groups who oppose each other quite openly. Also, those who claim to be followers of the 'line of the Imam' sometimes draw swords against one another.

Those who claim to act for the benefit of the Islamic Republic or to follow the policy of 'neither East nor West' are often so divided among themselves that nothing but a hostile relationship can be attributed to them. In fact, it cannot be said that they have differences of opinion, for they are exactly at the opposite side of one another. Therefore, taking into account that each of these groups finds some followers for itself, we see that our society resembles the society at the time of 'Ali.

Introduction by the Author

The importance of the Nahjul Balaghah then lies in two dimensions. First, it speaks about the fundamental of Islam such as the matters concerning God, the human being, Islamic views of humanity, prophethood and its position in human history, the dignity and prophethood of the Prophets and other matters which are today, a means of understanding Islam and thus necessary for us to study. Secondly, the Nahjul Balaghah refers to the social problems of a hypocritical society with which we deal today.

Accordingly, this book can be a source of Inspiration for us as regards the social and political problems of life and the possible solutions to them.

The fourth point about the Nahjul Balaghah is that a great number of its sermons are unfortunately incomplete, i.e. either from the beginning or from the end of each sermon some statements have been omitted. Even, in some cases, Sayyid Radi has omitted statements from the middle of a sermon and then continued the rest of it with the phrase "and from that", which is what the journalists and reporters do repeatedly today.

Now, we know nothing about the omitted parts and this creates some difficulties in interpreting the content of the Nahjul Balaghah. The reason why Sayyid Radi has made these omissions is that the Nahjul Balaghah (The Peak of Eloquence), as its name indicates, has been compiled from an artistic point of view, i.e. eloquence of expression.

This does not mean, however, that he has been heedless of the subject matter and has merely paid attention to the artistic aspects of ''Ali's Sayings. Yet', this eloquent man, one of the great Arab poets of his own time, has dealt with the Nahjul Balaghah with a poetic outlook. He has endeavored to pick out All's most beautiful and eloquent words and statements just as one tries to choose the best distich of a sonnet. This is why a type of semantic disconnection is observed among the statements of some Sermons.

Introduction by the Author

It is to be noted, of course, that both the highly eloquent and non-eloquent Sayings of 'Ali carry very magnificent purports, and it is these purports which make us appreciate the Nahjul Balaghah, now, in the fourteenth century (A.H.) more than a great scholar of the fourth century (Sayyid Radi) did. As a matter of fact, the human being has naturally faced so many hardships in the course of centuries that he or she understands ''Ali's words and message and the call of Islam from his tongue more easily than those who lived centuries ago.

It is important, as well, to know that when Sayyid Radi was compiling ''Ali's words and sayings, there were few people who valued All and his words as much as you value them today. Thus, a minority only followed ''Ali's lines of thought.

On the other hand, those people who took care of 'Ali's Sayings and tried to compile them, attached more (or at least equal) importance to the form and beauty as to the content of his statements and omitted some parts which they considered less beautiful than others. If you were Sayyid Radi you would definitely not treat ''Ali's words in this way. You would instead, try to benefit more from the contents of ''Ali's sayings. This is why we believe that today 'Ali and his words are more appreciated than in the fourth century, and this is why history is moving towards All and his message, something that we should accelerate.

The main subjects of the Nahjul Balaghah, which we are going to discuss in this book, are as follows.

Fundamental Beliefs

A part of Nahjul Balaghah is about monotheism, humanity, the Last Day, prophethood, Imamat and other fundamental principles of Islam. Of course, contrary to the manner of the dialecticians in the third and the fourth centuries, these subjects have been discussed in the Nahjul Balaghah with a kind of mystical and spiritual approach. Thus, the words of all about monotheism, for instance, are quite different from the words of Nasir al-din Tusi and other Islamic philosophers and theologians.

Introduction by the Author

Social and Political Matters

These matters consist of both general and specific social affairs including the administration of or Islamic country, the relation between governors and subordinates, letters to the rulers of different states (the famous letter to Malik Ashtar, for instance), the, way of facing the enemy, decisiveness free from improper hate and revenge, treating both friends and enemies exactly as they deserve, being not subjected to credulity and naivety and many other social matters of that time and of the whole history.

Morality

The training and purification of the human being's soul are among other subjects discussed in the Nahjul Balaghah, which we shall, God-willing talk about in the coming pages.

Lesson One: Prophethood (*Nubuwwah*)

Prophethood is among the subjects which have been dealt with in the Nahjul Balaghah and a discussion about which can help us understand one of the basic principles of Islam. In fact, it is not only a subject which can be followed throughout the Nahjul Balaghah but one of the most important and fundamental principles of Islamic ideology.

I have repeatedly mentioned in various discussions that in order to analyze and understand the numerous matters of Islamic thought and ideology, the principle of prophethood is an axis around which these matters can be discussed as well. As to the principle of monotheism, we believe that its social and revolutionary dimensions can only be clarified when we discuss it within the vast spectrum of the matters concerning prophethood.

Accordingly, our method in this chapter is to point out and analyze the different dimensions of prophethood and to support our discussion with an explanation of ''Ali's ibn Abi Talib's sayings wherever necessary. In this manner, two aims will be fulfilled, i.e. some important sections of the Nahjul Balaghah will be translated and interpreted, and issues among the basic Islamic principles will be made apparent.

It is to be mentioned at the beginning that in the discussion about prophethood, revelation and its relevant matters will not be discussed. Rather, prophethood will be viewed as a historical reality and an unquestionable event. Undoubtedly, prophethood has existed as a phenomenon in the history of mankind. There is no difference of opinion in this regard between us and those who disbelieve in it.

However, the difference lies in the interpretation of this event and the message it conveys. In fact, no one denies such personalities as Moses, Jesus and other Prophets whether or not the history of their lives is more or less known or vague. History reports that all of them have existed.

Lesson One

following questions will be answered in the analysis, which follows:

1. What was the social background (social, temporal and historical situation) when this event occurred?

2. Where did this event originate? Did it appear among the kings, the oppressed, the scholars and thinkers... which class of people?

3. What position did it enjoy? Was it to the benefit of a special class of people? Was it directed towards material advantages? 'Was it directed towards mystical and spiritual aspects of life? What was its social and intellectual direction?

4. What were the pros and cons when the Prophet first offered his message? Who were those who opposed it and to which class of the society did they belong? What were their motives and means of opposition? Who were in favor of it and to which class did they belong? What

were their motives and how did they assist the Prophet?

5. What was the aim behind the message of prophethood? Was prophethood aimed at material welfare? Was it aimed at class distinction? Was it aimed at enhancing the level of people's knowledge and understanding? Was it aimed at opposing or accounting for the powers of the time?

6. Did the Prophet call the people? Was it 'monotheism' with its social, political, economic and revolutionary dimensions?

Answering these questions, with regard to Islamic texts and records, will shed light on different aspects of this social reality and will acquaint us with a vast scope of Islamic thought. Of course the Nahjul Balaghah will be the axis of our discussion, although different verses of the Holy Qur'an as well as mental reasoning may be of great help both in answering the questions and in interpreting All's words.

Lesson One

The first question which is relevant is "What grounds were available for the manifestations of prophethood?" What was the social, economic and historical setting for the appearance of the Prophets? And among which class of people have they appeared? The Nahjul Balaghah has answered these questions on several occasions. In the first sermon, speaking about monotheism, the creation of heavens and the earth, the angels and other matters, the appearance of the Prophets and the background to prophethood in general are discussed as well.

We read the preceding sentence so that the connection to this matter is made clear.

From his progeny (Adam) God chose prophets and took their pledge for His revelation and for carrying His message as their trust. In the course of time, many people perverted God's trust with them and ignored His position and took partners along with Him. Satan turned them away from knowing Him and kept them aloof from His worship.

Then sent His messengers and series of His prophets towards them to let them fulfill the pledges of His creation, to recall to them his bounties.[3] the last part of this quotation reveals some peculiarities of the community in the 'Age of Ignorance', in which Prophets were sent by God to people. These peculiarities are hereunder explained.

It says that 'in course of time many people perverted God's' trust. The Holy Qur'an speaks about 'ahd on several occasions, examples of which are given below:

"Thy Lord has decreed you shall not serve any but Him" (17:23)

"Made I not covenant with you, children of Adam, that you should not serve Satan - surely he is a manifest foe to you?" (36:60)

"...And God made them testify concerning themselves, 'Am I not your Lord? 'They said,' yes, we testify... " (7:172)

---

3 Ash-Sharif Ar-Radi, the Sermons of ʻAli (Tehran: World Organization for Islamic Services, 1979), part one, page 19.

These verses imply that God's covenant ('ahd) is to abstain from servitude to Satan, that man's servitude should be exclusively for God and that human beings have primordially admitted that they are servants of God and should serve Him alone.

This is the meaning of 'ahd (trust and covenant) to which the Commander of the Faithful refers in the Nahjul Balaghah. In fact, he says that most of the people broke their allegiance with God and disobeyed His commands by worshipping idols, taking partners (holders of power and possessions) along with Him, imposing themselves on other people as worship-deserving idols and perverting the divine decree through ignoring or exclusive obedience to God.

It was under these conditions, the Commander of the Faithful asserts, that God brought about prophethood and appointed His Prophets. This is also emphasized in other statements of the first Sermon after describing the appearance of the Prophet of Islam and not the appearance of the prophets at large, although the social conditions and mental atmosphere in which all the Prophets, including Abraham, Moses, Jesus and others, have appeared have been the same, and thus what is said about the Prophet of Islam fits other Prophets as well.

"The statements run as under the people of the earth at this time were divided in different Parties, their aims were separate and their ways were diverse. They either likened God with His creation or twisted His Names or turned to other than Him...,"[4]

It says that the Prophet was appointed to prophethood at a time when people were divided in groups with different ways of thinking, i.e.. a universal mentality did not govern the is minds of all people, which indicates the lack of an acceptable culture at that time, separation among people and, finally, ignorance. It continues with the statement that 'their aims were separate'.

This has two implications. The simple one is that in different parts of the community or in different corners of the world people enjoyed

---

[4] Ibid. p. 20.

desires and manners of there own. The members of each community or class of people favored something, which the members of other classes and communities despised. In fact, the society at large lacked a common aim and aspiration, which shows the decline of that society.

The second implication is that there was not more than a few poles of power throughout the world at that time, and they were Sassanian Kings, Roman Emperors, Ethiopian Sultans and other despots, dictators and idols who stood at the peak of their communities, ruling over the people with tyranny and according to their own aims, desires and self-centeredness. The existence of insufficiencies and oppression in the Iranian community, the existence of impenetrable classes among the people, the boundless mastery of Brahmans, aristocrats and soldiers over the lower classes and the existence of moral, cultural, economic and class tyrannies, the pressure of which tortured the people, were all a manifestation of the sensuality and selfishness of the idols (kings) who possessed the leadership of the Iranian community.

Thus, the whims and desires of a minority dominated all the affairs of a majority of mankind.

"They likened God with His creation". It implies that those people who, according to their nature and spiritual feelings, believed in the existence of a deity and a creator, found it in the form of creatures and small, imperfect beings. Some of them worshipped cows as their gods. Others worshipped stone or wooden idols. In fact, all the people were in some way or another worshippers of God as their nature demanded but they were devoid of a perfect knowledge concerning God. This was the most manifest perversion.

"They twisted His Names or turned to other than Him». This was a kind of mental deviation prevailing among the believers of God. They were actually so involved in the Name of God that they could not take step beyond it. In ancient times, for example, those who had a vague view of God in their minds, being unable to know God perfectly, turned to His Names Allah, Mannan or Ilah and worshipped them. They were ignorant of the reality of God.

Another example can be observed in the extremist ideologies of today. Advocates of these ideologies claim to believe in God but if they are asked what God is, they cannot explain the true concept and meaning of this word. Rather, they take the 'whole existence', the rules governing nature and the cause and effect, conventions current in nature and history to be a god. They lack the ability to know the real meaning of God, i.e. to know Him as an independent 'Necessary Being' who is undoubtedly the Creator of this universe rather than being Himself the universe. They cannot perceive this reasonable, philosophical concept. Thus, they are confused about the Name and the real Being of God.

Naturally, wisdom, love, knowledge, spiritual attractions and moral Attributes, all of which originate from monotheism and a knowledge of God, do not develop in them and, therefore, prayers, incantations and the wise prayers of Imam Sajjad, peace be upon him, for example, become meaningless to them.

Accordingly, what such people worship is 'God' as a word without being concerned with its meaning and concept. This is a sign of the decline and deviation of religious as well as a characteristic of the people who lived at the time when Prophets appeared.

In the second Sermon, the Commander of the faithful has more detailed statements concerning the social background to the appearance of the prophets. They run as follows "At that time people had fallen in to vices whereby the rope of religion had been broken, the pillars of belief had been shaken, principles had been sacrileged, systems had become topsy turvy, openings were narrow, passages were dark, guidance was unknown and darkness prevailed. God was being disobeyed. Satan was given support and Belief had been forsaken.

As a result, the pillars of religion fell down, its traces could not be discerned, its passages had been destroyed and its streets had fallen

Lesson One

into decay. People obeyed Satan and tread his paths. They sought water from his watering places. Through them Satan's emblems and his standard was raised in vices, which trampled the people under their hoofs, and treaded upon them with their feet. The vices stood on their toes (in full stature) and the people immersed in them were strayed, perplexed, ignorant and seduced as though in a good house with bad neighbors. Instead of sleep they had wakefulness and for antimony they had tears in the eyes. They were in a land where the learned were in bridles (keeping their mouths shut) while the ignorant were honored."[5]

This is a very beautiful and artistic picture (in the form of an ordinary lecture from the pulpit) of the social conditions in the age of ignorance, in which the Commander of the Faithful portrays the adversities, deficiencies and disorders casting shadows over the people's life- the people who were mentally bewildered and perplexed and who did not know the aim and purpose of life.

---

[5] Ibid. p. 30.

We can easily and clearly understand the meaning of these words of his, because they provide us with an exact portrait of the situation of our own time, when the Iranian nation was severely oppressed and fell victim to the tyrannies brought upon it by the Pahlavi executioners and American mercenaries. In fact, what in this Sermon and other Sermons have been expressed about the background to the appearance of the Prophets (which the writer used to interpret consciously in connection with the situations of strangulation at the Pahlavi time conforms exactly to the conditions under which we lived during the Pahlavi rule).

In those days, especially in the last three years of the Pahlavi reign, the people were so mentally deceived and misled that they got on the buses and trucks in many cities, applauded, played the flute and shouted, "Long live the Shah". Meanwhile, the awakened conscience of a group of people was severely wounded; yet, this was not the common conscience of our community, for even those who refrained from participating in such shows, whether they were government employees, clergymen of other classes of people, accepted the ways and procedures of the ruling regime by their indifferent and apathetic behavior towards the prevailing situation.

The people were actually bewildered and dead. No one was aware of the aim behind his daily labor. They worked day and night but they were ignorant of the aim, aspiration and the future for the achievement of which human beings endeavor. The similitude of them was the like similitude of the 'mill donkey' that constantly moves in a circular direction and never reaches an end.

They were endowed with the best dwellings and lands, having all the God-given bounties and with the territory of human conscience, faculties and beauties, which have been hidden but now have bloomed in our revolutionary boys and girls, fathers and mothers. In fact, such a blessed background existed in people but the 'neighbors were bad' in the words of the Commander of the Faithful, i.e. the rulers and holders of power were incompetent and dishonest.

On the whole, under such conditions, which he recounts in the above-quoted statements, and we experienced in our own time, the Prophets were appointed to prophethood. We shall, God-willing, give more details about the background to prophethood, as pointed out in the Commander of the Faithful's words, which are very important so far as the philosophy of history is concerned, and which is misunderstood by some deviated individuals who draw wrong, material conclusions on the basis of their incorrect analysis in this regard.

Questions and Answers

Q. What is the difference between prophethood (nubuwwah) and appointment to prophethood (ba'tha)?

A. Appointment to prophethood is the sudden resurrection and awakening of an individual or a community of people who have plunged into the sleep of negligence, ignorance and bewilderment. Prophethood is the principal factor of the appointment, i.e. after the necessary competence and readiness is found in someone to connect with god and

Lesson One

the Divine revelation then he is appointed as a prophet. Thus, the appointment is the consequence of prophethood.

Q. Is "Ali's view a universal one, applicable to all communities such as the corrupt western ones? Are these communities subject to destruction without anyone saving them?

A. Yes, it is applicable to all communities at all times. But it should be added that at a time when the chain of prophethood ends in the Last Prophet and no one is appointed to prophethood any longer, it is the religious scholars as heirs of the Prophets who will lead the people and save human communities from destruction.

Q. Are, the signs, which Hadrat 'Ali provides us for the appearance of the Prophets the same as the signs, which we have received concerning the appearance of Hadrat Mahdi?

A. Concerning Hadrat Mahdi, mention should be made of the fact that before his reappearance the world will achieve a relative perfection. In fact, the universal government of Mahdi would be a perfectly just government. You and the coming generations before his reappearance should provide half of this justice. Today, due to the establishment of the Islamic government of Iran, which conveys a remarkable percentage of the message of Islam in this strategic region of the world, we have approached nearer to the reappearance of Hadrat Mahdi.

Q. It is true that all these signs are existent in our Revolution and in the whole world. Is the reappearance of Hadrat Mahdi possible in this period?

A. Yes, it is possible. But another thing, which is quite possible, is the decline of the superpowers of the world and the appearance of new movements and resurrection, which we have pointed out repeatedly. This is because the world has entered a new period with the advent of our Revolution, a period in which the deprived of the world and the weak nations will no more remain indifferent to the tyrannies of the great powers, will stand against them and will finally demolish them as a small animal can destroy a huge elephant by mounting its ears.

Lesson Two: Background to Prophethood

In the previous lesson, the background to the appointment of the Prophets was discussed with regard to a few statements of the Nahjul Balaghah. This lesson is aimed at completing what was mentioned before by analyzing in detail the peculiarities of two periods, which are of concern in our discussion, i.e. the pre-Islamic period or the 'Age of Ignorance' (the period before the appointment) and the Islamic period (the period after the appointment).

The Age of Ignorance

According to ''Ali's words, in the Age of Ignorance, the people suffered from two kinds of inadequacies: material and spiritual.

Material Inadequacy

In this period, the level of social welfare and security was very low. This is explicitly expressed both in the Nahjul Balaghah (in different sermons) and the Holy Qur'an. The

Qur'an refers to the Age of Ignorance saying (106:4).

Spiritual Inadequacy

Spiritual inadequacy is the very ignorance and bewilderment of the people, i.e., they are devoid of a clear way of living and an aspiration for life. It is, in fact, a great suffering for man and society not to seek a sublime aim in life but only to try to provide for the daily requirements and necessities. Unfortunately, this state of living was characteristic of the 'time of strangulation' (Pahlavi reign), when life was without any aspiration and the best and most active individuals, in the eyes of people, were those who made their utmost effort to enjoy a life of welfare or those who did not have any involvement at all but spent their time in lewdness and buffoonery.

Generally speaking, the middle class, i.e., traders, workers, housewives, university students and others were all endeavoring to provide for the ordinary requirements of their lives. The similitude of them was the similitude of the car, which refuels from one gasoline station to another gasoline being a means for it to constantly go from station to station.

In fact, the people worked in order to gain their daily bread, which enabled them, in turn, to work again. They actually spent their lives in eating bread and gaining bread. This state of living cannot be perfectly felt by the idealist youth of today who have specific aims and aspirations in mind, who work for the establishment of the true Islamic government and who seek the fall of the superpowers. It is the existence of these aspirations in the society of today which reveals the spiritual inadequacy (lack of aims and aspirations) of the society during the Pahlavi rule.

Society during the 'Age of Ignorance', i.e. before the appointment and revolution of the Prophet, was likewise an aimless and deviated society. The people were bewildered. They turned round themselves just like the 'mill donkey' that permanently turns round the millstone, perhaps traversing ten or fifteen kilometers a day, but never moving more than a short distance away from the mill. They were ignorant but more ignorant than them were those who followed destructive aims and aspirations, which, if realized, would destroy them as well as the whole community.

In this regard the Holy Qur'an says:

"Hast thou not seen those who exchanged the bounty of God with unthankfulness, and caused their people to dwell in the abode of ruin? -Gehenna, wherein they are roasted, - an evil establishment!" (14:28-29)

In fact, all the holders of power and authoritative rulers of the world, all the great capitalists who commit any crime to establish their vast economic networks and all those who have brought about great corruption upon the earth in the course of history can be categorized among the spiritually deviated people with destructive aims and aspirations.

To say the least, it was in such a deviated society and among such a misled people that the Prophets were appointed to prophethood. The most outstanding characteristic of such a society is the alienation of man which causes the development of material aspirations in a group of people who follow the aim of making material, monopolies and increasing the rate of material products which, in turn, results in the poverty of other people.

The Commander of the Faithful says, "I never saw an ample blessing (wealth) unless beside it I saw a trampled right." Poverty gives rise to class distinctions which bring about deeper gaps among the different classes of people and causes other problems such as the unjust division of social authority under which rich classes gain more power than others, although money is not always efficacious in gaining power, but sometimes social power, too, is effective in making use of money and creating material monopolies.

Thus, both social and economic factors are influential in the appearance of tyranny, exploitation, ignorance and deceit in a society where perverse and destructive aims have replaced noble aims and aspirations.

This is where Islamic analysis and material analysis come face to face, for according to materialists, mental possessions, beliefs and whatever comprises one's soul, mind and thought originate from one's 'class position' which includes the social, economic and even the cultural dimensions of life, whereas the Islamic viewpoint is that the origin of all pressures and adversities existing in a society results from the dominance of ignorance and alienation in that society. Islam says that it is alienation which brings about class distinctions and which divides society into two classes, i.e. the oppressed and the oppressors.

Spiritual alienation is, therefore, an outstanding characteristic of the Age of Ignorance and the Prophets appear, in effect, to lead the people to the straight path and to remove their spiritual depravities. This is what the Commander of the Faithful emphasizes in the second Sermon of the Nahjul Balaghah which was previously mentioned and which is hereunder reviewed and explained in detail.

Lesson Two

He says, "I also stand witness that Muhammad, peace and the mercy of God be upon him and his descendants, is His slave and His Prophet, sent him with the illustrious religion, effective emblem, written Book, effulgent light, sparkling gleam and decisive injunction in order to dispel doubts (shubuhat) present clear proofs ... "

Shubuha is the plural form of 'shubha' and means doubts and differences of opinion, which exist, in the human mind and thought as regards truth and falsehood. These doubts and differences appear, as far as the people's beliefs are concerned, when the society at large goes astray. In fact, society comes to believe that it lacks reality and to disbelieve the most manifest realities.

For instance, during the rule of the previous regime, the people had come to believe in and accept 'monarchy' which was an untrue phenomenon, and had completely forgotten a clear and undeniable reality named, 'Imamat'.

Thus, the Prophet was sent by God to remove mental doubts and errors and to "present clear proofs," as the Commander of the Faithful says i.e. to save people from the perplexity of philosophical reasoning by offering them clear proofs. This does not mean, however, that such reasonings are basically useless and philosophy must be abandoned.

Some people today, find fault with Islamic philosophy, the classic philosophy of Islam on the false basis that it is mixed with Greek philosophy. They insinuate that Islamic philosophy is mixed with Aristotelian philosophy.

They do not realize that Islamic scholars and philosophers, centuries ago, cleansed Islamic philosophy of Greek philosophy. Moreover, they are unaware of the fact that a philosophy with a heavenly world-view cannot be mixed with a philosophy having a material world-view, although they may share some common aspects.

Thus, philosophy should not be abandoned, although philosophical reasoning is not very effective in awakening and provoking people

Lesson Two

at a time when a revolution is to be conceived. At such a time, only the clearest proofs and reasoning's can make the people aware of the prevailing situations, the wrong ways upon which they step and the right path they should choose.

This has been the manner of all Prophets of God. They called people to the belief in the One God. They called them to their nature and to their natural beliefs, without exposing them to ordinary, spiritual reasoning's.

In the case of the Islamic Revolution of Iran the reasoning's of the intellectuals for fighting the West never contented the least number of people because the intellectuals themselves were not satisfied with their own reasoning's due to the fact that they never made their appearance in the battle arena, whereas the words and lectures of the Imam Khomeini, which contained clear realities concerning the dependence of the tyrannical regime of Pahlavi on the superpowers and the prevention of the society from practicing their religion (Islam), doctrinal beliefs and worship, could be perfectly understood by the people, and finally resulted in that great movement in our society. It can be concluded, therefore, that the Prophets presented clear proofs and reasoning's which not only elicited but also which the middle class of people could understand and then follow naturally.

The Commander of the Faithful continues to enumerate the tasks of the Prophet saying, administer warning through signs and to warn of punishments.» In fact, he means that the Prophet came to acquaint the people with the signs of chastisement and with the punishments, which happened to the past nations in the course of history, and to tell them that they would also be afflicted with the same punishments if they followed the manners of those nations.

Then he portrays the situations during the Age of Ignorance (before the appointment of the Prophet) and points out the troubles and calamities which endangered the minds, hearts and the spirituality of the people, which blocked the ways of guidance to them and which led them astray - the troubles which did not have anything to do with the material life and apparent welfare of the people.

He says "At that time, people had fallen in to vices, whereby the rope of religion had been broken, the pillars of belief had been shaken, principles had been sacrilege, systems had become topsy turvy, openings were narrow, passages were dark, guidance was unknown and darkness prevailed. God was being disobeyed. Satan was given support and belief had been forsaken. As a result, pillars of religion fell down, its traces could not be discerned, its passages had been destroyed and its streets had fallen into decay."

The general message of these words is that the society in which the Prophets were appointed to prophethood was devoid of guidance and the Prophets' mission was to lead the people to the straight path so that they could forsake the state of indifference prevailing among them and seek good aims and aspirations.

As was mentioned before, should a motive more sublime and nobler than eating, drinking and providing for the ordinary requirements of life become dominant in the people's efforts and endeavors and should destructive aims and aspirations forsake society, then social, political and economic conditions will prosper, class distinctions will vanish and the idols of wealth and power will be smashed.

This was experienced during early Islam, at the time of all the Prophets and even in our own revolutionary society (if the opponents let us finish this experience). This is why we believe that our Islamic Revolution has rendered useless all the social, political and revolutionary formulas which support the idea that movements and revolutions originate from material motives, class distinctions and class quarrels in societies which have apparently political systems of their own and which are not subject to colonial rule (like Iran during the Pahlavi regime).

Lesson Two

What happened in Iran was exactly the experience of the Prophets, i.e. the people who lived in a mentally-perverted society were awakened by factors of guidance and hurried towards their natural promise to worship naught but God, to appreciate God's plentiful blessings and to believe in their own social power.

Guided in such a way, these people who had for many years been subjected to the oppression and coercion of the so-called masters and kings, suddenly arose, revolted by the millions and brought about the Islamic Revolution. Today, to continue the Revolution and to guarantee its survival, it is necessary to keep the people's mental guidance intact in order to deepen their belief in God and Islam and to make them more aware of their human dignity and responsibility.

The Commander of the Faithful continues his Sermon with the following statements, providing more details about the mental and spiritual atmosphere of the Age of Ignorance (before the appearance of the Prophet). He says " ... People obeyed Satan and tread his paths. They sought water from his watering places. Through them, Satan's emblems flew and his standard was raised in vices, which trampled the people under their hoofs, and treaded upon them with their feet. The vices stood on their toes (in full stature) and the people immersed in them were strayed, perplexed, ignorant and seduced as though in a good house with bad neighbors. Instead of sleep they had wakefulness and for antimony they had tears in the eyes ... ".

In fact, he believes that the origin of all adversities, oppressions, corruptions, sufferings, disorders and crimes existing in society during the Age of Ignorance, resulted from obedience to the Satan's of the time who, with reliance on their social authority, i.e. wealth, power and deceit, wasted God's noble blessings and devastated the plentiful, vital resources of the time with unthankfulness and the transient lives of the people or exploited them for their own benefit, regardless of what happened to the real owners of those valuable resources.

It was on the basis of such obedience that the people went only the ways which the masters and dominant groups showed them, the ways which ended in no desired destination, which brought them nothing but increasing poverty, ignorance and captivity and which provided the dominant groups of society, i.e. the creators of evil, corruption and decadence, with their personal interests.

In the Islamic world-view, the human being is considered a thoughtful, innovative and independent creature. From these three characteristics, the power of thinking of the human being is more important than others, for it provides one with awareness, which enables one to move and make progress.

Thus, the most significant and fundamental factor for the movement of history and society are the knowledge and awareness, which stimulate human beings to action. It is awareness, which induces humanity to move and act. In the course of history spontaneous actions and movements have never resulted in a Revolution.

Maxim Gorki in his book, Mother, endeavors to prove that it was the labor movements which gave rise to the October Revolution in Russia, whereas a careful study of his book indicates that these blind movements could obtain no results. In fact, without the existence of awareness and guidance, the spontaneous movements brought about in the history of revolutions could never end in the desired aims.

Thus, class conflicts and wars, which materialists emphasize as the origin of all movements and revolutions, have not been effective at all. Rather, the most significant factor for the movement of history and society has been understanding, guidance and stimulating awareness. Without these, all actions and endeavors have usually ended in undesired effects, which can be observed in a great number of the revolutions throughout the world.

Now, since awareness is the main source of inspiration in societies in which ignorance is dominant, the antihuman elements (holders of corrupt authority), in order to retain their tyrannical system, have always tried to stifle any liberating thought by exposing people's minds to stupefaction and poisonous instructions and to destroy the origins of consciousness.

As a result, in such societies, the people follow only the desires of these satans, learn only what they teach and, like sheep, go only towards the water to which they are led by these treacherous shepherds ("they sought water from his watering places").

It is quite painful that, in the light of the sacrifices and endeavors of the oppressed people, those who stand against the oppressors and criminals are usually defeated and killed, while the chiefs of the atheists are rarely killed. For instance, Mu'awiya, the manifest example of blasphemy, never accepted ''Ali's call to challenge him in person because, as a Satan, his emblems flew through the deprived people who have always been employed in the course of history as a ladder which the arrogant have climbed to approach their self-centeredness, dominance and power.

The life of the deprived has always been blended with fear, anxiety, confusion, poverty, hunger, ignorance, disgrace and lack of awareness. This has been an out standing characteristic of the ages of ignorance. But according to the principles of our religion and Islamic ideology and according to the Holy Qur'an, which says, "We have honored the children of Adam, human beings are honorable. In fact, the belief in the Oneness of God is followed in Islamic thought by the dignity and worth of human beings.

Generally speaking, those societies in which human beings are honored because of believing in God and having will-power, and not on the basis of their social positions, move towards perfection and prosperity; while those societies which grant no worth to human beings and their thoughts do not tread the path of improvement and goodness and are usually administered through dictatorship.

Today, other than the Iranian community upon which Islam has shed its light, all human communities throughout the world are ruled either by black strangulation (such as the socialist communities in which the Proletariat dictatorship is dominant and the so-called supporters of the labor classes, i.e. their leaders, have never felt the hardship and poverty of the laborers) or by despotism prevalent in such despotic countries as Egypt, Iraq, Saudi Arabia and so forth.

There are, however, other communities (Western ones) which are ruled by the stupefaction of the people, i.e. keeping the people amused with passions, sexual matters, alcoholic drinks and other means of corruption and adversity.

It is only the Islamic community, which establishes equal rights for all the people, whether they be workers, physicians or peasants. But that very Islamic community will keep aloof from Islam, should decision-making, judgment and awareness be confined to a special class of people (whoever they might be) and others is compelled to follow them blindly.

On the whole, what the Commander of the Faithful says is that in societies which are dominated by ignorance and alienation, although humility and worthlessness cast shadows over all human aims and aspirations and hunger, horror, disease, captivity, corruption and bewilderment threaten the society, the people are surprisingly tolerant and in agreement with the oppressors. This is what he calls sedition and calamity (fetna), something that brings a person to the state of consternation and deception, which causes damage to one's heart and mind and which destroys one's life completely. It is, in fact, under these circumstances that the Prophets appear.

They do not appear merely to remove poverty, to establish social welfare, to eliminate ignorance and to teach the people how to read and write. But each of these is a part of a great whole, which comprises the aims of the Prophets. The Prophets' aim is to eradicate human deviation, alienation and bewilderment and to give one spiritual elevation. The realization of this aim will, however, be followed by material welfare, social security, eradication of ignorance and class distinctions and so forth.

Questions and Answers

Q. You said that alienation gives rise to class distinctions. Now what are the causes of alienation?

A. The cause of alienation is the lack of the use of the power of thinking, for this faculty can be effective only if it is trained, educated and used properly. It is just like a very powerful projector, which can offer its sparkling nature only if it, is clean and not covered by dust and mist. The power of thinking may lose its usefulness under the influence of various factors, the most important of which being whims and passions.

Of course, other spiritual factors as well as the holders of worldly power are also effective in this respect, but material and economic factors alone should not be regarded as a basis for lack of thinking and alienation. Thinking is the faculty by which the human being analyzes different matters and comes to a general conclusion. It is, therefore, independent and can provide people with reasons concerning their doings.

Q. In one of his sermons, 'Ali says, "I shall bring out the truth from falsehood.» How do you interpret the leftists' justification of the 'dialectic conflict' on the basis of this statement?

This statement cannot justify A. 'Dialectic conflict'. By this statement he implies that he can analyze a collection of saying in which right and wrong have been mixed, distinguish the right from the wrong and introduce it to the people. This is the art of all the thinkers who know the truth.

Q. What is a classless, monotheistic society? Is monotheism and class not two contradictory notions?

A. A classless society is one in which there is no legal distinction among different groups of people and all the individuals are provided with equal rights and opportunities. In such a society, every individual makes efforts in accordance with one's physical and mental faculties and whatever one earns belongs to one's self. No one has the right to ask another for a part of what one has earned. Of course, if an individual kept a long distance from others, that person would be advised to assist them. Islam holds equal possibilities and opportunities for all individuals.

Every one has the right to educate one's self, to enhance one's knowledge, to take one's desired job, to work in the best possible manner and so forth. At the same time, lazy people are not permitted in Islam to have a share in what hardworking people acquire. In Islam the people are free to work and endeavor for themselves, contrary to socialist communities in which all productive jobs and services are a monopoly of the governments and thus being wrongly called classless.

As to the 'monotheistic society', it should be stated that it is a society in which all the people stand at the same level so far as legal, judicial and social laws and regulations are concerned. In a monotheistic society, there is no difference between the ruler and a layman before the law. A Jew and a Muslim are equally treated (the judge calls 'Ali and the Jew to his presence and addresses both of them in the same manner).

A monotheistic society is an Islamic society and a classless one is also Islamic but only within the limits, which were explained above. We do not believe in the classless society, which Marxists define. We do not believe in what they call class, classlessness and class war. These are all Marxist concepts which the group of so-called Mujahidin (the anti-Islamic group of hypocrites) have mixed with Islamic notions to deceive people. To say the least, society should either be called 'monotheistic', which is in conformity with Islamic culture, or classless (as defined by the Mujahidin) which reminds one of Marxist ideology.

Q. Are all human beings equipped with equal talents and faculties?

A. No, not all human beings enjoy the same talents and faculties and not all of them are equal in understanding different matters and performing various tasks. In fact, every individual has a talent for certain types of work and no one is found to be devoid of certain gifts and talents.

Lesson Three: To Which Class Of Society do The Prophets Belong?

In this chapter we are going to discuss the social origins of the Prophets themselves, i.e., to find out the social class to which the Prophets belonged. We are going to see whether they belonged to the rich people, aristocrats and holders of worldly power or to the poor, the needy and the deprived. It is, in fact, very important to know the social and economic classes from which the Prophets have arisen in the course of history, founded monotheistic movements and revolutions and provided the masses with divine words and messages.

The Holy Qur'an, the Traditions and the Nahjul Balaghah are rich sources, which can help us in the analysis of this matter, but here the emphasis is only on the words of the Nahjul Balaghah. In the long and famous sermon of al-Qasi'ah (the Sermon of Disparagement) there are statements which deserve careful reflection and which offer information concerning the matter being discussed.

The statements run as follows: "certainly, if God were to allow anyone to indulge in pride, He would have allowed it to His selected prophets and vicegerents. But God, the Sublime, disliked vanity for them and liked humbleness for them. Therefore, they laid their cheeks on the ground, smeared their faces with dust, bent themselves down for the believers and remained humiliated people (they were from the oppressed people). God tested them with hunger, afflicted them with difficulties, tested them with fear, and upset them with troubles."[6]

Here, the Commander of the Faithful speaks about pride and vanity and emphasizes that since God disliked these two qualities; He misrepresented them in the eyes of His Prophets and righteous beings. Therefore, the Prophets hated self-deceit and superiority complexes, but liked humbleness and humility. Thus, they bent themselves down for the believers, lived among the lowest

---

[6] Ibid. Part two, page 406. Parenthesis is the translator's.

classes of the people, rubbed their faces with the dust (in prostration) before God and refrained from indulging in haughtiness. They did, in effect, what the Holy Qur'an orders to be done to the parents. It says:

"... and lower to them (one's parents) the wing of humbleness out of mercy ... " (17:24)

The Prophets, according to the Commander of the Faithful were from the oppressed masses of the people. They knew the, pains and agonies of the needy. They felt, for instance, what hunger was, because God had tried them with hunger. The Holy Qur'an quotes Moses, peace be upon him, to have said:

"Oh God! I need what you shall send me."

According to narrations, Moses, peace be upon him, was hungry and implored God in this manner to send him bread so that he could satiate his hunger. Thus, the Prophets felt the pains of hungry people. They had tasted the sufferings of life. They knew well the troubles of hard physical labor in cold and hot weathers. They understood the meaning of hardship.

Timidity and the state of being fearful are characteristics of the oppressed. They are usually fearful of the future, poverty and the dominance of a powerful hand over their destinies. They are always worried and in a state of mental disturbance, concerning the existing situations and the coming conditions. They expect at any moment to be put under pressure by a Powerful oppressor.

Likewise, the Prophets suffered from such fears and anxieties and, to say the least, were so surrounded by hardships and difficulties as to become pure in the same way as gold derives its purity under the pressure of very hot temperature. In fact, the Prophets were not pampered individuals to suddenly come Out of their Palaces and call the people to make a revolution.

There was a close link between them and the common people. They had, like all members of the society been subjected to ignorance, tasted the pains and sufferings of life and then became worthy to be called 'Prophets'.

The Definition of the Deprived (*mustad'af*)

A society dominated by ignorance is always made up of two groups of people. One group consists of those who make Plans, administer society and have total authority over all affairs. The other group consists of the subjects and subordinates who have nothing to do with different affairs of society. They work hard (and thus they are not good-for-nothings as they are usually called, compared for example, to the amount of work Pharaoh performed with the slaves in building the Pyramids), but they have no right to apply their will, personality and points of view in the administration of the affairs of their society.

The first group is a minority consisting of the powerful families and dynasties with various degrees of authority over society. They are called 'the arrogant' (mustakbirin). The second group are the common people and the masses who are regarded as the weak and who are devoid of authority whatsoever.

They are called 'the deprived' (mustad'afin). Our own country, during the corrupt regime of Pahlavi, was administered by a limited number of individuals, with the Shah at the head of them. It is true that an institution named the 'National Consultative Assembly' existed but all the decisions were made by the Shah and his American advisers and dictated to the members of the Assembly, who had no will of their own.

At the lower levels, the big money makers who acted in collusion with governmental personages, by governor-generals and so forth, made decisions. In fact, the total authority was centralized in the hands of one person, the Shah. If all the ministers, Assembly members, director

Generals and the like agreed on something, but the Shah opposed; it was his will and decision, which prevailed. The rest of the people, i.e. the masses, had no authority (even over their own destinies) to interfere

Lesson Three

with the affairs pertaining to foreign relations (with Russia and America, for instance), internal industries, agriculture, animal husbandry, etc. let alone matters concerning religion and morality. They had no right to meddle with the total course of affairs of their society due to the absolute lack of democracy, voting and elections in the country.

This state of affairs is nowadays an obvious characteristic of all socialist countries but in a more respectable form, i.e. one party (the Communist Party) possesses the total power and authority in administering the affairs of these countries. In fact, the high governmental cadres, supreme councils and the general secretary himself determine all the affairs of these countries. Other people have no right to express their viewpoints, and their will and decisions are not taken for granted. Thus, mental development is repressed in such countries, and perhaps this is why the youth usually engage in Sports and physical training and blossom out as the first rate athletes in international competition such as the Olympics as we observed in the recent Olympic games held in Russia.

In western societies, too, the situation is more or less the same (mostly in the so-called civilized countries of America and Europe where 'freedom' and 'democracy' have widespread literal application). Nowadays, there are unfortunately some people who try to transform freedom and democracy to western conceptions of freedom and democracy, without knowing that the West itself is bereft of real freedom; (in America, West Germany and the likes, people imagine that they elect their representatives freely whereas the reality is that it is specific currents which lead them to one side or another to cast their votes in favor of one party or another. Recent elections in America and the conflicts between the Democratic and Republican parties are the best evidence, verifying this reality).

Generally speaking, in all countries of the world, people are divided into two classes: the deprived and the arrogant. The deprived masses are themselves two groups: the needy and the non-needy. In fact, a poor and wretched peasant who performs fifteen hours of physical labor a day under the difficulties of rain, snow and hot weather and one who lives an ordinary life, being a shopkeeper, or employee, etc., without suffering so much, are both in the category of the deprived, because both of them are considered to be worthless and good-for-nothing and are devoid of the right to participate in the administration of their society.

According to the Commander of the Faithful in the quoted Sermon, the Prophets belonged to the deprived classes and, like them, have been deprived of the authority to carry out a responsibility in their society. A historical review of the life-accounts of Muhammad, peace and the mercy of God be upon him and his descendants, and other Prophets will clarify this matter further.

Moses, peace be upon him, was born to a deprived family among the children of Israel who lived under severe pressures. But after birth he was brought in a completely arrogant house and became a favorite with the Pharaoh's family although he had not been born of the Pharaoh's wife.

He was brought up under the best living possibilities, the most delicious food and different kinds of luxuries (as a perfect aristocrat). Then, when Pharaoh noticed that he was nourishing an enemy within his house, Moses decided to escape. In fact, Moses had begun his invitation and calling people to God, had started his revolutionary propagations within the royal palace and had succeeded in converting the Pharaoh's wife to submission to God when Pharaoh experienced a feeling of danger and decided to prosecute him. Moses escaped to Egypt.

To say the least, Moses became a Prophet and invited the people to make a revolution when he was within the royal house and at the peak of arrogance (this biographical account of Moses is narrated in the Qur'an, and no use was made here of the Traditions).

Our Prophet, Muhammad, peace and the mercy of God be upon him and his descendants was born in a tribal house of high rank. He was the grandson of and a favorite with 'Abd al-Muttalib, the chief of Mecca (although he was, unlike Pharaoh, a pious, chief and a believer in God). When his father, Abdullah, who was one of the dearest children of 'Abd al-Muttalib, died in youth, the latter brought up Muhammad, peace and the mercy of God be upon him and his descendants, until he became four years of age (although Moses was the favorite with a great emperor and Muhammad with a tribal chief, both of them enjoyed the favor of highly respectful families).

Then 'Abd al-Muttalib passed away and Muhammad came under the guardianship of his uncle Abu Talib who did not enjoy the same respect as his father, 'Abd al-Muttalib, but who was himself a distinguished personality, not belonging to the masses.

Abu Talib acted as a good guardian for a period of time and then he was afflicted with poverty. Thus, Muhammad lost the (financial) support of his uncle at this time. But before long he married Khadija, a rich woman. He first acted as a functionary to Khadija but later on, (fifteen years before his appointment to prophethood) he married her, thus becoming a relatively rich man in Medina.

The very financial state remained with him until he became a Prophet at the age of forty (this is why it is said that Islam advanced through Khadija's wealth and "Ali's sword).

Accordingly, the Prophet of Islam was born to an aristocratic family and lived a comfortable and affluent life until God appointed him to prophethood. After the appointment, however, due to the high expenses of propagation and calling people to monotheism and due to the lack of opportunity for conducting business, he became poor.

Other prophets, too, were more or less wealthy. It is in the Traditions (although there is no clear, historical accounts available) that Job, for example, possessed lands, gardens and trees which were destroyed when God wanted to test his belief. David, too, had a rural origin. He was a commoner. Yet he became a commander and a ruler. Solomon was born in the house of this commander (David).

In fact, this chosen Prophet of God (although there is no difference between him and Moses as far as his purity, piety, revolutionary spirit and prophethood are concerned) was the son of a ruler. Abraham was born in the house of an idol-carver, and the history of nations and religions reveals that idol-carvers were not only not among the low, deprived classes but were also considered to be saintly and respectable.

We come to the conclusion, therefore, that a considerable number (not all of them) of the Prophets have been brought up among affluent and powerful families. Thus, we have two points here to be considered along with each other: First, in the Commander of the Faithful saying that Prophets have belonged to the deprived and humble masses of the people. Second, the Prophets (some of them), as we see above, have been born among the socially, comfortable families of high ranks.

Are these two realities incompatible? No It is not the main point here to see whether they are compatible or not, The main point is to nullify the (communists') imaginary legend that all the revolutionary agents have originated from the proletarian, bare-footed and needy classes. What is essential is that a revolutionary person (be he a leader of the revolution or a commoner) should be dressed with revolutionary morals and Attributes.

Materialists and the interpreters of Marxism, in fact, hold a wrong belief that only those individuals can enjoy revolutionary morals and Attributes who themselves belong to the poor, bare-footed or proletarian classes, for man is always and everywhere a human being and thus corrigible. He can, like the Prophets about whom 'Ali says, "They were from the deprived people," equip him with correct, revolutionary habits and with the attributes of the deprived.

Lesson Three

It is true that aristocratic training and education entail no result but an aristocrat human being, yet it is untrue to believe that such an education (in a person who is brought up in an aristocratic atmosphere) is unchangeable and indestructible.

In fact, should divine guidance (either in the form of thinking, meditation and the awakening of conscience of the individuals themselves or through training and purification of the soul by the teachers of morality, i.e. the Prophets) enlighten the sick bodies of those who are under the influence of aristocratic habits and training, they would come out of their spiritual depression and become dressed with revolutionary dispositions.

Summary

Two points are perceived when the social origin of the Prophets is put to discussion: First those who are appointed to prophethood are dressed with the Attributes of the deprived, revolutionary morals and combative spirit against the existing class systems of the arrogant, i.e. at the time of the appointment (and even before it) they have an anti-arrogant position in support of the deprived.

Second, having these Attributes does not necessarily imply that all the Prophets belong to the deprived classes. They can either belong to these classes or not but, as was mentioned before, even at the time of appointment to prophethood and at the beginning of their revolution they may belong to the arrogant strata, having a comfortable life. There is no need for them to have suffered from forced labor and hard work before the appointment. Of course, they should have felt pain and distress but this does not necessarily mean that they should curtail the bonds of relationship with their social class and their (comfortable) life.

Spiritually exalted Beings Have Understanding as Well as the Feeling of Sympathy.

Subsequent to the discussion concerning the arrogant and the deprived, it should be added here that such a class division does not exist

Lesson Three

in monotheistic societies. It is, in fact, the exclusive characteristic of' societies suffering from ignorance and alienation. We have of course, rulers, ruling classes, caliphs, holders of religious authority and governments in monotheistic societies but none of them are arrogant enough to manage the affairs of these societies on the basis of personal beliefs.

Also, there are commoners in such societies, consisting of workers, businessmen, peasants, bricklayers, government employees and so forth, but none of them arrogant either. Each class has, in fact, some authority over its own social affairs in proportion to the total number of its members.

For example, under the present situations of Iran (although Iran is not a 100% or even 50% Islamic society at the present time), every individual has some authority and the right to vote as a member of a society with thirty-six million individuals.

It is on this basis that the great movements and even the political affairs of our country are nowadays managed and led by the people themselves, although it may be considered wrong so far as the prevailing patterns of politics on the international level are concerned. The truth is that if the people were not inclined towards certain actions and policies, connections and disconnections, the government (itself consisting of Muslims belonging to the low classes of people) would not dare take such positions as it does today and perform such courageous actions. This is indicative of an Islamic country (although Iran is still not a perfect Islamic country).

When Islam shall, God-willing, shed its light on our society in all its dimensions, the role of every individual in the administration of the whole country will be to the extent that he or she (although being the lowest in social position) can act and promise on behalf of the Islamic community. Today, if a given government or a certain action be condemned in the sermons of the Friday ritual prayer in front of a multitude of people, or if a treaty between our country and a given government be orally made (or violated) in such sermons, neither our own government nor the addressee will take care of it.

But in a perfect Islamic community, there is no irresponsible individual. In such a community, in which Islamic culture and education are perfectly dominant, every individual (being a businessman, a housewife and so forth) can conclude a treaty or announce an agreement for the cessation of hostilities or a special occasion and the Islamic government is obliged to take it into account, although that individual not be a minister, an army commander or a diplomat. In fact, every individual can decide for the whole community on specific occasions, and all accepts his or her decision.

This is not, however, practicable under the present culture and habits of our society. But as the society gets closer to Islam and its teachings, this is more likely to be accomplished. It should be added, of course, that when we say something is not for the time being practicable, it does not mean that Islam as a whole cannot be materialized. It can, but only when the world has a complete readiness for its acceptance.

Questions and Answers

Q. You said that Khadija's wealth and "Ali's sword made the progress of Islam possible. Does this not lead to a deviating concept that wealth and material things have been the only factors for the spread of Islam?

A. We do not believe that wealth alone played a role in this regard, but the truth is that wealth, too, had certain roles and this is undeniable. It was, is fact, necessary for the satiation of the newly converted people's hunger as well as for providing the expenses of those who were sent here and there by the Prophet. This does not negate the influence of the spirituality and dynamism of Islamic thought and ideology, since the very dynamism is in need of material things when acting and making progress in the same way as it needs physical labor and activity.

Q. You defined the deprived in its social and political aspects. Is it not necessary to explain the economic and cultural aspects of it as well?

A. The economic activities of the deprived (as previously defined) are also under the influence of the powerful, i.e. economic activities are usually centralized where power is centralized (under the previous regime of Iran, for example, no productive and economic activity took place except through the direct or indirect interference of the government).

Therefore, economic aspects are dependent on political aspects. It may, however, be argued that political power originates from economic power. This is possible but it lacks universality. Sometimes political power is the cause for the absorption of money and sometimes money gives rise to political power.

They are inter-connected, but in a society wherein political power is centralized in a certain group, economics cannot grow and progress independently. The cultural aspects (culture in its prevailing, not in its revolutionary sense) of society, too, are affected by the opinion of those who possess political and economic power. Thus, when political oppression dominates society, the existing cultural and political aspects of the deprived are also influenced by It.

Q. Is the following tradition, narrated from the Imams concerning deprivation, authentic? "The deprived are those who endeavored in the way of God but could not achieve their aim in establishing the divine system. The highest of them are the Prophets and saints, next to them are the believers who make efforts in the way of God."

A. It may be authentic for all the Prophets and their true followers belong to the category of the deprived.

It provides us with the definition of the deprived not with the concept of deprivation.

Lesson Four: How are Prophets Chosen?

What are the Prophets' responsibilities towards God? What is the social, cultural and intellectual background in which the Prophets appear? To answer these questions, we analyze the following statements of the first Sermon of the Nahjul Balaghah. "From his progeny (Adam), God chose (istafa) Prophets and took their pledge for His revelation and for carrying His message as their trust."

Istafa (to choose the best) is a very important and fundamental issue. In Arabic, not all selections are indicated by this word. Only when a pure element is recognized and chosen from amongst a collection of elements is the 'istafa' used. It is actually employed when the pure and the impure are separated in a collection of things and the pure portion is extracted.

As far as physical and spiritual aspects of humanity are concerned, the Prophets have been ordinary human beings but, at the same time, they have possessed the competence needed for gaining high ranks and positions. Accordingly, they have been selected, distinguished individuals, born of parents none of whom have been involved in polytheism and human Corruption Thus 'istqfa' in its general sense implies that a trained and educated Generation deliver a more trained Generation to society.

As an example, the Prophet of Islam was born in a pure and holy family, from a father and mother who were, in turn, distinguished from the point of spirituality and morals (and not on the basis of race, blood, wealth and aristocratic privileges). In fact, 'Abdullah was superior to all fathers and Amina was superior to all mothers. These two spiritually trained beings married and provided society with a child nobler to all children, a better spiritually trained being.

So much is certain that the Prophets who appeared before Moses; peace be upon him, enjoyed lesser spirituality than those who came after him and after Jesus Christ, peace be upon him, for every Prophet has been the product of the training and education brought by the Prophets before him, i.e. the prevailing divine and spiritual training provided by past Prophets have been quite influential for the growth of the coming ones. Thus, the Commander of the Faithful uses the word 'istafa' to indicate that God has appointed those beings to prophethood that have had this spiritual training.

And took their ledge for His revelation and for carrying his message as their trust." Here the Commander of the Faithful mentions the Prophets' commitments and says that they are committed in two respects: First they have a commitment towards the divine revelation, meaning that they are obliged to say merely what they receive as revelation and not to intermix their personal views with the divine message.

Second, they are obliged to deliver the message they have received and not to bury it with themselves.

In the course of time many people perverted God's trust with them and ignored his position and took partners along with Him.

Satan turned them away from knowing him and kept them aloof from his worship." In five short sentences, the Commander of the Faithful provides us with a precise account of the mental, practical, social and cultural background of the people at the time of the Prophets' appearance.

In the first sentence he uses the Phrase 'aktharu khalqihi' (the majority of His creatures) to indicate that not all the people, but a great many of them, had perverted God's prescription and commands because absolute darkness or ignorance has never had dominance over a society, that is, in no age and era People have been left without heavenly guides, teachers and messengers who have themselves had some faithful followers.

In tact he refers to a society and a time in which people ignored God's orders, changed the general principles delivered through the chain of prophethood and deviated the course and program of life determined by the Prophets through the application of prejudices, perversions and Personal grudges.

Lesson Four

He continues with the phrase 'facahiluhaqqah' (thus they ignored His Position), meaning that people forgot about God's power and providence in administering the affairs of society (the same situation is dominant today among the westerners who do not feel the absence of God in their lives, because they have remained far away from their true nature. They have forgotten the existence of God although they apparently believe in God and hear His name repeatedly. They actually do not know God's Position and status in society).

What is God's trust and covenant (ahd)? Almighty God has provided human beings with a general pattern of life and a specific course within which people should move. This course or pattern is the very reality to which all the Prophets have invited people throughout history, i.e. monotheism, respect for humanity and moral, natural and legal quality of human beings. This is the divine program, a command and covenant.

Satans try to pervert this course and command and to induce people to obey and worship God's creatures instead of God. God calls people to honor the human being and satans invite them to humiliate and belittle him. Thus, the perversion of the divine covenant is to deviate from the mentioned course and pattern, to ignore God's position and to transform society into a satanic one in which partners are taken along with God.

Taking partners along with God is not merely confined to worshipping an object. But when God's position remains unknown and the people do not know that creation and Legislation belong to God (i.e. in the same way as the laws of creation - laws relating to the movement of heavens and the earth, day and night, man, birth and death - are in possession of God alone, Legislation or administration of the society and life, too, is under His authority. This is the meaning of God's position in human life).

They accept certain lines of thought as their guide, certain human beings as their rulers and certain false customs and traditions as their manners of living. They thereby replace God with ignorance, unawareness and satans

Lesson Four

(which only in our limited minds are regarded as rivals to God for, in reality, God has no rival). For example, Egyptians were actually taking a Pharaoh like Anwar Sadat as a partner along with God when they left their destinies in his hands.

The Commander of the faithful continues with the statement, "Satan turned them away from knowing Him.." to emphasize that when God's position remains unknown in a society, satans try to fill up the human mind, which is bereft of the knowledge of God in some way or other.

Sometimes one lacks something and he knows that he lacks it, but more painful is the case when one lacks something and he knows it is not due to the fact that the empty place of what he lacks has been filled with something else of his thirst has been quenched with muddy water. (This is the greater oppression the victims of human beings, i.e. suppression of man's God seeking sense or imposition of unawareness on man). Later on we shall see that Prophets have the responsibility to remove this oppression and compensate for it.

It is to be noted here that Satan (shaitan), referred to in ''Ali's sermon, should not be mistaken for Iblis, the creature who, according to the text of the Qur'an, refused to bow down to Adam and then implored God to keep him alive till the Day of Judgment but God promised only to keep him alive, until the Day of the Time Appointed. This creature should not in any way be assimilated with other creatures. We should grow accustomed to accepting the exact concepts of the Qur'anic statements, and not merely what our prejudices warrant.

Satan has a different meaning. Generally speaking according to the Qur'an, it is applied to those forces, which, create corruption, wickedness and deviation. On this ground, we have in the Qur'an" satans among men and jinns», i.e. satans among humankind who put on clothes, walk and do the like, and satans of the kind of jinns. These satans who sometimes dwell within the human being and are called selfishness, carnal desire, avarice, Aggression, negligence and so forth. Sometimes they dwell outside the human being and are titled king, ruffian refractory, corrupt religious leader, aphrodisiac scene, etc.

Now, should we not develop satans within ourselves, outside satans cannot influence us. For the very reason we cannot put the blame of our own deviations on social conditions or on those who have led us to negligence. It is in the Qur'an that the arrogant and the deprived will quarrel on the Day of Judgment. The deprived accuse the arrogant of having misled them but the arrogant deny it and argue that they themselves should not have listened to them. Both of them tell the truth and at the same time, both are condemned.

"... And kept them aloof from His worship."

By this statement the Commander of the Faithful means that when human beings do not know God, it is quite natural for them not to worship Him and not to serve Him (servitude is submissive action before God).

Summary

God has chosen the best of His servants (istafa) as His Prophets.

He has bound the Prophets to two responsibilities: To tell people only what they received as revelation and to hide not any part of revealed matters.

At the time of the Prophets' appearance, the people had taken partners along with God due to lack of knowledge concerning Gods position, and thus satans had led them away from God - seeking course towards the negligence of God.

Lesson Five: Duties and Responsibilities of the Prophets

In the previous lesson, it was concluded that the chosen Prophets of God have certain responsibilities towards God and the people. This lesson is aimed at discussing these responsibilities.

Our discussion here does not include such matters as the establishment of a monotheistic society and a prophetic government, not meaning that these matters have not been part of the Prophets' missions.

They have definitely been aimed for and the Prophets have come to establish the ideal society for mankind).

If fact, responsibility or mission here means the change that the Prophets bring about within the human being, for founding a just, monotheistic society is impossible without constructed human beings in the same way as a social revolution is inseparable from an inner revolution among people.

This change and provocation originate from the heart of the Prophet, encompass the hearts of people and finally lead to inner explosions among the arisen and faithful individuals. Should the means of such provocation be available (for which the Prophets are responsible) then it would be time to construct society and establish the monotheistic system.

Now, we will study the Prophets' responsibilities in the following words of the Commander of the Faithful "Then God sent His Messengers and series of His Prophets towards them to help them to fulfill the pledges of His creation, to recall to them His bounties, to exhort them by preaching, to unveil before them the hidden virtues of wisdom and show them the signs of His Omnipotence..."

With this general policy, the Prophets connected themselves with the people and their inner selves. i.e., with these aims and manners of developing human beings in their mind, they began their missions and on these same bases they tried to establish the Islamic community. Thus, in all dimensions of the Islamic community such as education, economics, government, human relations, etc., nothing contradictory to these aims should be found.

For example, if in an Islamic community something creates forgetfulness instead of 'recalling', that is against the philosophy behind the Prophets' appointment to prophethood. In fact, all the social signs of an Islamic system, i.e. all those things that constitute the minor and major structures of an Islamic community, should induce people to "fulfill the pledges of His creation".

These five programs (to which the Commander of the Faithful refers) were compensatory for the deficiencies existent among people during the age of ignorance when Prophets were absent - deficiencies and short comings mentioned in this same Sermon, which we analyzed before under the title 'mental, social and ... backgrounds to prophethood' ("In the course of time many people perverted God's trust with them...").

What is this 'trust' or 'covenant'? It is the human being's absolute servitude towards God, the human being has a commitment towards God and that is worshipping none but Him. Worshipping other than God means submission to others, whether it be mental, physical, doctrinal or practical. The human being is actually responsible to submit to no one except God but this does not mean that one has accepted this responsibility without having had power and a free will to reject it. The human being's nature and one's inner mechanism conform to the servitude and worship of God. These are, in fact, hidden in humanity's primordial nature. The Holy Qur'an says:

"Made I not covenant with you, children of Adam, that you should not serve Satan - surely he is a manifest foe to you? And that ye should worship me, (for that) this was the straight way?" (36:60-61)

After appointment, the Prophets ask human beings to destroy the change and distortion which they have brought about in God's trust and to make contact with God on the basis of their covenant with Him ("fulfill the pledges of His creation". This is the very removal of deficiencies of the age of ignorance, the age in which 'God's position remains unknown', the age when Prophets come to recall God's bounties to people.

Asking people to fulfill their natural covenant with God is not a complementary matter. It has a general and, at the same time, absolute concept involving propagation through mere speaking, providing the addressee with final reasoning and teaching purification of the people through controlled behavior. In the Holy Qur'an we read

"Invite (all) to the way of thy Lord with wisdom and beautiful preaching; and argue with them in ways that are best ..." (16:125)

In this verse, God asks the Prophet to expose the simple minds of the people and the adversaries to wisdom at the beginning stages and after a firm foundation for reasoning is achieved, guide them by preaching. These results in the purification of the mind and soul and, as the final stage, prevent them from establishing wrong reasoning, argue with them and convince them.

Concerning their relationship with human beings, Prophets are obliged and responsible to remove mental obstacles. Thus, those individuals or regimes that bring about such obstacles are opposed and fought by the Prophets. Accordingly, the Prophet's asking the people to fulfill their natural covenant ranges from wisdom and reasoning to the Islamic jihad (religious and spiritual struggle in the way of God for the removal of the obstacles.

The 'natural covenant' and humanity's primordial nature (i.e. worshipping God alone) are in conformity with the natural structure of the whole universe. Therefore, all the decrees and regulations of the Divine Law, which are incumbent on human beings, conform to human nature. This is clarified in several verses of the Holy Qur'an. Examples are as follows,

Lesson Five

"So set thou thy face steadily and truly to the faith: (establish) God's handiwork according to the pattern on which He has made mankind: no change (let there be) in the work (wrought) by God. (30:30)

In Sura Ar-Rahman, some of the verses speak of humanity's structure and Attributes and of the time of creation such as:

"(God) most Gracious! It is He who has taught the Qur'an... He has created mankind..."

Some others refer to natural phenomena such as the following,

" The sun and the moon follow, courses (exactly) computed; and the stars and the trees - both (alike) bow, in adoration. And the firmament hat He raised high, and He has set up balance (of justice..." (55:5-7)

It should be noticed here that by 'bowing in adoration' the Qur'an implies that natural phenomena are in a state of submission towards God and move according to specific rules and regulations. It should also be observed that the, balance, has nothing to do with plants, sun, moon, etc., but exclusively for humanity's good and evil deeds to be recognized and measured.

Then the Qur'an continues,

> *"In order that ye may not transgress (due) balance. So establish weight with justice."*

This means that human beings should not violate the laws of creation (natural laws) and religious laws, which are in a state of balance and conformity. Accordingly human beings are obliged to maintain this practical connection with nature (i.e. natural laws).

Thus, when human beings or the community move against the Divine Law and regulations, they are actually moving against the primordial nature of humanity and the world. And the Prophets come to bring this 'natural covenant' (covenant with God which originates from humanity's heart and warrants a kind of harmony between one's actions and movements and the structure of the Universe) to the stage of action.

Lesson Five

Another duty of the Prophets, according to the Commander of the Faithful is to recall to people the forgotten bounties of God. Human beings forget many of God's bounties and blessings; the most important of which being one's 'self' which is the axis for all God's blessings.

We read in the Qur'an:

"And be not like those who forget God, and whom He hath therefore caused to forget their proper selves." (59:18)

One's 'self' (that great but forgotten blessing), despite being not more than one thing, has various effects and manifestations. Thus, forgetting it is to forget those tools and means by which one can attain knowledge and recognition means of thinking, means of decision-making, means of innovation and means of accepting responsibility, the lack of each, damages one as a human being. By means of thinking and the power of analysis, one acquires knowledge and understanding and finds the ways. And through one's 'free will' one has the ability to choose.

Now when one distinguishes the right way from the wrong and chooses it, one can perfect the self through innovation and disclose the dead-ends. In fact, lack of innovation and initiative prevent one from going the way of perfection and making progress in the fields of culture, civilization, industry knowledge and morality. Finally, when one consciously chooses the way, one becomes responsible. A person confronts cases in which one should act as well as cases in which one should refuse to act. If one does not understand the case well and if one lacks free will to choose, one will have no responsibility. But if one understands it well and one has freedom of choice, then a person will be responsible.

On the whole, in an ignorant society, human beings forget one or all of these four characteristics, and the Prophets came to recall to them what they had forgotten. This is why the empty-handed and uncultured people who are reminded by the Prophets of their own 'self' and, as a result of their beliefs in God, they can stand firmly against the most stable political systems and gain victory.

The Commander of the Faithful enumerates the duties of the Prophets, saying, "to exhort them by preaching...". The Prophet is responsible to propagate his message; otherwise, revelation remains a monopoly with him and, thus, two dimensions of prophethood are left unrealized. The Holy Qur'an affirms this

"And remember God took a covenant from the people of the Book, to make it known and clear to mankind, and not to hide it..." (3:187)

Should the Prophet not fulfill this responsibility, the problems related to prophethood will remain unsolved. This is also true with an Islamic community in which propaganda plays a great role. In fact, it is not Islamic if a community falls short in propagating the message of God.

The Commander of the Faithful continues, «to unveil before them the hidden virtues of wisdom», meaning that the Prophets should call people to thinking, contemplation and wisdom which all human beings possess in their nature.

The power of thinking and contemplation may be weak in a community and land or among a Generation not necessarily because of geographical conditions, racial deficiencies or stupidity but due to the fact that powerful classes and seekers of dominance prevent people from correct thinking and stop the development of minds by different means (such as the wrong systems of education, prevailing nowadays in underdeveloped countries, which cause minds to be accustomed to various formulas and remain undeveloped due to lack of necessary practices).

As was mentioned before, the power of thinking is a property common to all human beings. But sometimes it is buried (by customs and traditions or by ruling systems) and made a treasure from which no benefit is derived, a treasure hidden behind the curtain of whims and fancies, false imaginations, legends, distorted matters and absurd ideas under the name of religion, philosophy and science.

In fact, the holders of power, wealth and deceit (kings, priests, pseudo-theologians and the wealthy) dispossess human beings from the power of thinking or do not provide them with the means for the development of thought (this is the very colonial program enforced in colonialized countries).

This is where the Prophets arise and unveil the treasures of thought and wisdom, inviting people to contemplation. This is observed in the following verses of the Qur'an, which call people to think about the most common phenomena of the world and to see in them the wonder, which is usually hidden from the eyes of human beings.

"Do they not look at the canals, how they are made?" (88:17), "Then let man look at his food (and how we provide it)..." (80:24)

"For what we pour forth water in abundance and we split the earth in fragments." (80:25-26)

These events and phenomena to which the Qur'an refers are quite common and familiar to human beings, yet when they contemplate them, their minds gradually develop and become active. This development of the mind is clearly seen in the Islamic community during early Islam when Muslims arose 'n a short period of time from the depths of ignorance and short sightedness to such heights that they soon came to be known as the founders of experimental sciences and great universities.

Another task that the Prophets fulfilled and to which the Commander of the Faithful makes a reference is "and show them the signs of His Omnipotence", meaning that they provided the people with manifestations of the divine power. This is what he himself does in this very Sermon[7], i.e. he refers to some examples of the heavenly signs to persuade people to think about them.

He continues: His Omnipotence, namely the sky which is raised over them, the earth that is placed beneath them, means of living that

---

[7] Sermon No. 1.

Lesson Five

sustain them, deaths that make them die, aliments that turn them old, incidents that successively betake them.

What is this ceiling (sky) over our head? It is a collection of air, space, stars and so forth, to which we have grown accustomed, yet something that provokes us to think what it really is and, as a result, provides us with understanding and recognition. Newton acquired the very recognition concerning a great reality by paying careful attention to a natural and very common incident to which no one before him had contemplated.

He simply asked why the things did not go up but rather fell vertically down when they were freed in the air, and subsequently he discovered the powerful force of gravity. In fact, all scientific progress and developments in the field of astronomy have originated from the very attentiveness to which the Prophets always called the people.

What is this bed (earth) beneath man's feet? What has it been created from'? What is beneath it? Where would we reach, should we excavate the earth? These are the questions from which such sciences as geology, mining, etc., originate.

What is the food, which maintains life? How is it prepared? Why is it needed and why should we try to obtain it? What is living with all its aspects such as speaking, walking, eating, etc., and what is death and becoming lifeless and silent'? What causes one to grow old? Why is one happy and glad at one stage of life and exhausted, weak and disable at another stage? The answers to these questions and the careful study of such events and phenomena (life, death, youth, old age etc.) induce human beings to employ their minds and activate them. This is why the Prophets have to show the signs of God's power to the people.

Lesson Six: The Continuity of Prophethood

Continuity is one of the main points in the discussion of prophethood. In the first Sermon of the Nahjul Balaghah, the Commander of the Faithful aims at picturing the line of prophethood as a consistent and continuous line in the course of history extending to the time of the Prophet of Islam.

In fact, never in the course of history has there been a time or place devoid of a Prophet or signs of a Prophet in the past, i.e. either a Prophet has lived among people appointed by God to provide them with good tidings or to make them fear (God's wrath) or there has been something left behind by a Prophet, which the people obeyed as they obeyed the Prophet himself.

Thus, believing in the fact that the earth has never been devoid of a 'proof' (of God) does not necessarily mean that in a given nation or community, a Prophet has always lived who has been immediately taken, over by another Prophet at the time of death. It rather implies that after a prophet's death and before the advent of the next prophet there was something (a book or a faithful disciple), which the people followed and obeyed as the successor of the dead Prophet.

In the Arabian Peninsula, for example, it took a very long time before the Prophet of Islam appeared. There was a long transition between the disappearance of Jesus Christ, peace be upon him and the appearance of Muhammad, peace and the mercy of God be upon him and his descendants. In Sermon No. 88 of the Nahjul Balaghah, the Commander of the Faithful points out this matter saying, "God sent the Prophet when the mission of other Prophets had ended and people had fallen into".

Now we pursue our discussion concerning the continuity of prophethood with regard to his words in the Nahjul Balaghah. In Sermon no. 1 he says, God never allowed His creation to remain without a Prophet (nabi) deputed by Him, or a book sent down from Him or a binding argument (proof) or a standing plea.

Lesson Six

The difference between nabi and rasul is that a nabi merely receives the message from God but a rasul in addition to receiving the message, has the mission to propagate it and deliver it to the people. This is, of course, not totally acceptable because the aim of receiving a message is nothing but propagating and the deliverance of it to others. However, we might suppose that a nabi takes the message but it is not the time to deliver it, just as the Prophet of Islam received the message (revelation) on the 'Night of Power' "We have indeed revealed this Message in the Night of Power." but it took twenty-three years before he could fulfill the duty of conveying it to the people.

In the Sura Ta Ha, verse 114, the Holy Qur'an addresses the prophet, saying:

> *"... Be not in haste with the Qur'an before its revelation to thee is completed".*

Accordingly, nabi mursal (the deputed prophet), as the Commander of the Faithful puts it, is referred to as a Prophet who actually conveys his message to the people.

What is the meaning of 'Kitabun munzal (a book sent down)? Does this sending down refer to a place? The fact is that to send down a book actually means to transform the book into letters and words (language) which humanity understands, i.e. to adapt the high heavenly concepts and realities to the level of one's thoughts and understanding.

In fact, God, the exalted, inspired the Prophet with the highly complicated facts and learning's in the form of the most simple words and expressions which could be understood by all and which later came to be called the Qur'an, just as a teacher simplifies difficult matters and gives them to his students.

This comparison may, however, be wrong, for in any case there is a logical and ordinary connection between a teachers' mind and heart and those of his students, whereas there is a great gap between an ordinary man's heart and the divine lofty teachings.

The Commander of the Faithful asserts that in the absence of Prophets and heavenly

Lesson Six

books, there was either a 'binding argument' (an unfading proof by which people could convince the enemies) or a 'standing plea' (a clear and permanent way) on which people could depend.

On the whole, every nation in the course of history has enjoyed one of the following: First a Prophet (like Moses, Jesus, Abraham, etc.). According to a Tradition there has been 124,000 Prophets, the first of them being Adam and the last one being Muhammad, peace and the mercy of God be upon him and his descendants.

Second, a heavenly Book, left behind by a Prophet. In this very Sermon (Sermon No. 1) he speaks of the Last Prophet, saying, "... The Prophet left among you the same (the Book) which other Prophets lefts among their peoples..." By 'Book' he means a collection of written teachings and commandments, which all the Prophets possessed. Some of these books were, however, descended to the Prophets themselves (these are not more than a few) but others were those left behind by previous Prophets, either distorted or misunderstood, which the Prophets after them undertook to correct or interpret.

As an example, after Moses, the Torah was misunderstood by some, even mingled with polytheistic ideas, and thus such Prophets as Salomon, David, etc., who succeeded Moses, tried to provide the people with the true meanings and concepts of this Book.

This is also true with the Qur'an. That is to say that there is a considerable difference between our understanding of the Qur'anic teachings and that of the past generations (taking into account the fact that the text of the Qur'an and its concepts and realities have remained untouched). In the past, these teachings were considerably misunderstood because distorted matters and wrong ways of thinking obsessed the people's minds and prevented them from the correct understanding of the Qur'an.

But today, the Qur'an is correctly understood and it is likely that in the future some Qur'anic realities be unveiled that we do not perceive today (According to some traditions, when eventually Imam-Mahdi reappears, he will introduce a new religion-the true Islam. Today, some Sunni and non-Sunni jurists have announced that the religion, which people follow in Iran, is not Islam.

They tell the truth because this is not that Islam in which they believe-that distorted Islam which contains idolatry, polytheistic and anti-Islamic ' values. Our Islam is different from that Islam whose mosque does the President of America inaugurate and whose Qur'an does the Shah of Iran print. There is a great and changing distance between these two forms of Islam).

The Books of the Prophets were, however, sufficient as long as they remained untouched, their concepts were rightly expounded and they were correctly interpreted. In the case of Moses, for example, his Book remained perfect and undistorted after he died, during the time when the Children of Israel were in a state of bewilderment and sought to reach Jerusalem, and guaranteed the victory of Israelites as well as the establishment of the Mosaic community.

(This community, which was powerful and enjoyed a government, came into being after Moses' death. In fact, Moses made preparations for the revolution and provoked the people but he did not live long enough to witness the establishment of his ideal community, and it was the people who accomplished this task). The Torah was actually preserved and kept aloof from distortion by the successors of Moses (Yusha ibn Nun and Kalib ibn Yuhanna) who succeeded in pursuing that heavenly, Islamic and monotheistic dynamism, i.e. the genuine Torah.

Third, a fixed and undeniable proof. This can be seen in the period after Jesus Christ ascended to the heavens (he was not killed), during which time Christians were subjected to manifold oppression; namely, the oppression of the Roman Empire whose foundations were based on polytheism, which severely persecuted the followers of this progressed monotheistic religion; and

Lesson Six

the oppression of non- Christian Israelites (the Jews) who did not believe in the Message of Jesus Christ.

As a result, Orthodox Christian Israelites lived for many years in concealment and in a state of strangulation without the opportunity to gather together or convey the prophetic legacy to one another freely. The famous disciples of Jesus Christ had to tolerate a great deal of distress in traveling between the cities and lands in order to propagate Jesus' Message.

To say the least, the prevailing state of oppression kept the true Bible of Jesus Christ far away different versions of this heavenly Book; namely, the four Gospels of Matthew, Mark, Luke and John, none of them containing the exact words, sayings and signs of Jesus Christ.

Thus, the original Book (the Bible) was not among the people, yet the existence of the Torah's commandments, which Jesus Christ had announced to be valid and practicable if modified, the existence of the mentioned calamities and the existence of Jesus' guidelines were all an undeniable proof preventing people from refuting the prophecy of Jesus Christ and provoking them to transfer Christian teachings to the coming generations who could, in turn, move and act on the basis of such teachings.

Fourth, a clear and manifest way, i.e. the means and decrees that are not found in the Book but the people possess. It is in a Tradition related from Imam Hassan al'Asgari, peace be upon him, in which he has explained the qualities and Attributes of Islamic jurisprudents. Someone asked the Imam why the learned men of the Christians and the Jews (priests and monks) are reproached in the Qur'an whereas the learned men of Islam are praised.

What is the difference between the two? The Imam gave a detailed answer, the epitome of which is that the learned men of Islam, too, are not unconditionally praised. They are praised provided they possess the Attributes that Islam has determined. But should they contrarily follow the same perversions and disgraces adhered to by priests and monks, they will also be blameworthy.

Priests and monks were actually dependent on the powerful and supported them. Although the realities had reversely been manifest in the people's eyes, they did not take action to provide the people with a true portrait of their religion. But the people could discern, on the basis of a series of natural (primordial) principles, the perverseness of the way to which they had been led.

Basically, at any age there is a set of accepted natural principles among the people, resulting from the continuous instructions of the Prophets in the course of centuries, which enables them to distinguish the truth from falsehood (for example, when a religious scholar or a man of God compromises with the enemies of God, it can be said without reasoning that he is in the wrong. It is quite obvious and natural that he goes the wrong way, for one cannot obey God and His enemies simultaneously).

People can, in effect, distinguish the right way from the wrong by a reference to their hearts and according to their intrinsic beliefs which are the very 'standing pleas' and manifest ways.

These four elements (this clear way) always existed in man's life before the advent of Prophet of Islam. It sometimes happened, however, that two Prophets were living at the same time in different corners of the world or two heavenly Books were followed by two different nations. But the important point was that heavenly guidance made its appearance in all places and at all times (even among the wild, primitive people). Yet, more important of the number of those who denied them never caused the Prophets to neglect fulfilling their obligations.

In Sermon No. 1 of the Nahjul Balaghah the Commander of the Faithful says, "These Messengers were such that they did have not feel little because of the smallness of their number or of largeness of the number of their falsifiers."

Lesson Six

In fact, none of the Prophets fell victim to disappointment but rather all of them succeeded in achieving their aims although the number of them was small (124,000 in proportion to the world population from the very beginning till now) and the number of their falsifiers was large. Falsifiers were the ones who spread out falsely the point that the Prophets' way, message and prophethood were wrong.

They were great in number and in some cases they even killed some of the Prophets. yet the Prophets never fell short in pursuing their general and ultimate aim, i.e. prosperous community, and never became hopeless in accomplishing their mission.

They not only struggled for the spiritual elevation of the people of their own time but they also tried to attain the total prosperity and historical evolution of human beings as a whole. And they were successful in this respect. Even those Prophets who were killed had the opportunity beforehand to convey their message and introduce their heavenly lines of thought, which although were kept hidden for some time, were finally unveiled and practiced again.

Muddarres, as a follower of the Prophets, had a message to convey at the time of the strangulation of Reza Shah's reign. He believed in the policy of, "Negative Equilibrium" or in his own terms "adami", meaning that we shall neither pay tribute to the West nor to the East. He said, "Religion should not be separated from politics." For the deliverance of such a social and political message, he was arrested, exiled and finally poisoned and choked by stuffing his own turban in his mouth (his grave is now besides a small farm in Kashmar).

He departed and was buried in the remote deserts, but gradually one of his beliefs, "Negative Equilibrium" (before the announcement of this policy by Muddarres, Russian and British governments were equally privileged in Iran. For example, in 1919, Vuthuq ad-Dulih granted the western part of Iran to Britain under a treaty. Russians objected to it, and he granted the north to them.«Positive Equilibrium») was revived eighteen or twenty years later, at the time of Dr. Mussadiq.

Muddarres, Sayyid Jamal (of Asadabad) and others, all being messengers of truth and justice and compassionate lecturers of their own time, were so devoted and courageous that they expressed their views and left behind their lines of thought. But it could be much better if they themselves could have the opportunity to materialize their messages in a better manner and could witness the overthrow of the Pharaoh and the freedom of the people after they had been exposed to so much trouble and distress.

However, their names, actions and messages are recorded in history despite their untimely death. They did not neglect their aims and duties and history will not neglect them either.

Questions and Answers

Q. Will Jesus Christ appear after the reappearance of Imam Mahdi?

A. Yes, the Traditions attest this.

Q. We know that the Torah and the Bible have been subjected to distortion. Why has the Qur'an been an exception?

A. It has been proved with sound reasonings that not even a "," (and) has been deleted from or added to the Qur'an. During the time of the third Caliph (Uthman) someone recited the following verse of the Qur'an but intentionally omitted the «,» before "alladhin" which changed the meaning of the verse to a great extent, implying that only those priests and monks who bury gold and silver are condemned, whereas the verse refers to two groups of people - priests and monks who devour the substance of men in falsehood and the people (they may be by priests and monks or not) who pile gold and silver. The verse reads as follow,

"O ye who believe! There are indeed many among priests and anchorites, who in falsehood devour the substance of men and hinder (them) from the way of God. And there are those who bury gold and silver and spend it not in the way of God. - Announce unto them a most grievous penalty ...
» (9: 34)

At this event, 'Abdullah ibon Mas'ud, who was present there, put his sword on his shoulder and said angrily, "If you do not recite the verse with the "," you deleted, I will secede from Islam." They were this sensitive. They themselves had heard the Prophet reciting the verses of the Qur'an and had recorded them in their hearts and writings and, thus, they preserved them at the expense of their life. In this way, the Qur'an, which came down to the Prophet was preserved in the original form by the retentives and recitors who permanently recited the Qur'an and kept it from additions and deletions.

Q. What is the difference between "bayyeneh" and "hujjat"?

A. Bayyeneh is a clear and manifest proof, which merely convinces a person, but hujjat is a proof or reasoning by which a person disputes with his enemies.

Lesson Seven: The End of Prophethood

"... Among them was either a predecessor who would name the one to follow or the follower who had been introduced by the predecessor." (Sermon 1, Nahjul Balaghah)

In the previous lesson, we mentioned that human beings have never suffered from the absence of the Prophets or revealed Books. Here in the above statement, the Commander of the Faithful points out that all the Prophets have had the same direction, although their followers stand against each other today (Jews against Christians and Christians against Muslims...)

He actually means that there have been no dispute or quarrel among the Prophets, all of them traversing the same path, conveying the same message and knowing each other quite well. Everyone of them introduced the Prophet after him and talked honorably about the one before him. For example, Moses informed his followers that Jesus Christ would be his successor and Jesus Christ mentioned, in turn, the name of

Moses. Thus, the disputes and wars running among the followers of the Prophets are quite illogical, originating from egotism and selfishness.

We see, therefore, that this situation (the successive coming of the Prophets, heavenly Books and the Prophets' followers such as the Imams) continued along with history and humanity's evolution till God appointed Muhammad peace and the mercy of God be upon him and upon his, descendants as the last Prophet.

In this regard, the Commander of the Faithful continues with the following words: «In this way, ages passed by and time rolled on, fathers passed away while sons took their places till God deputed Muhammad (peace and the mercy of God be upon him and his descendants) as His Prophet, in fulfillment of His promise and in completion of His Prophethood.»

What has God promised which should definitely be fulfilled? The answer can be traced in the Qur'an where it gives good tidings, in the words of Jesus Christ, of the advent of Muhammad, saying:

"And remember, Jesus, the son of Mary, said.- O children of Israel, I am the apostle of God(sent) to you, confirming the Law (which came) before me, and giving glad tidings of an Apostle to come after me, whose name shall be Ahmad. It is He who has sent His Apostle with Guidance and the Religion of Truth, that he may proclaim it over all religion» (61:69)

Thus, God's promise is the victory of Mohammed's religion (or prophethood) over all of humanity's intellectual courses and social experiences. This does not mean, however, that during the Prophet's lifetime this aim should have been achieved (as it was not achieved in practice due to the Prophet's departure), nor does it mean that the Prophet of Islam should, in the long run, overcome all religions, nations and schools of thought (although this has been realized many times in history and the Islamic government has approached a worldwide extent)

The proclamation of truth actually has a more delicate significance. In fact, the thought and mentality of human beings and their creativeness, initiative and innovation increasingly provide them with new ways and manners. Ideologies come into being, grow up and become widespread in this way, and thinkers and philosophers (such as Plato Socrates and ...) make their plans for humanity's social life or the basis of these new ways and manners.

Now, the path (school) of the Prophets will gain absolute victory over all the ways designed by human beings at a time when the whole content of the prophethood is given to the people. The path of Moses was certainly the path of God but no one claims that it was the most perfect path ever disclosed for humanity.

It was quite appropriate for the time of Moses but it lacked that much capacity to encompass various necessities of human life at all ages and times. It is likely that such man-made schools of thought shall appear in the course of the coming centuries as to be more perfect than the school (religion) of Moses.

Thus, Moses' religion was not the one to overcome all other schools and religions because the line of prophecy had not come to an end and the cup of prophethood had not overflowed. Moses filled a part of this cup and Jesus filled another part but they could not go forward because human beings did not have the capacity to absorb more. The people were, in effect, mentally weak. Otherwise, God would have bestowed on them the whole message of prophethood through His first appointed Prophet.

But when the people got the essential readiness, God deputed His Last Messenger to provide them with all (the knowledge and awareness) that could be contained in the human mind and to complete the culture of prophethood, fulfilling the divine promise and overcoming all religions and man-made schools of thought.[8]

---

[8] For a better understanding of this matter, refer to Martyr Murtada Mutahhari's The End of Prophecy.

The completion of prophethood speaks of the end of the line through which humanity connects itself directly with God, i.e. revelation. When this line comes to an end by the appearance of the Last Prophet there is no further need of revelation, Gabriel and so forth, because human beings themselves are thereafter capable of understanding new ways and manners of life and extracting them from what has been offered to them in a complete form by the Last Messenger of God, who stands at the end of the chain of prophethood.

Now, going back once again to the Nahjul Balaghah, we see that all the Prophets preceding the last, such as Noah, Abraham, Moses, Jesus and so forth, had a commitment to believe in him, as they anticipated his coming: The Last Prophet stood in effect at the peak of prophethood and other Prophets who were below him in rank had to await him, believe in him (i.e. believe in his prophethood and message) and love him.

The Commander of the Faithful says, "God deputed Muhammad (peace and the mercy of

Lesson Seven

God be upon him and his descendants) as His Prophet, in fulfillment of His promise and in completion of His Prophethood. His pledge had been taken from the Prophets, his traits of character were well reputed and his birth was honorable."

There is, however, a subtler significance in these statements and that is that the Prophet's commitment was neither a written nor an oral one. They had, rather, a natural and primordial commitment to heighten the thought and understanding of human beings and to make them ready for the advent of the Last Messenger.

This commitment is similar to the commitment of the teachers of lower grades towards the teachers of higher grades, although they may not know one another. In fact, the former are responsible to train the students' minds in such a proper way that the latter can make the more advanced matters and more extended concepts easily understood.

The Commander of the Faithful continues that the Prophet's «traits of character», i.e. his physical, familial, spiritual and behavioural signs and characteristics were known to one and all and thus a few number of people such as Salman of Fars could unprecedentedly, and without being exposed to his later teachings and programs, know him an come to a perfect belief in his religion. As to the birth of the Prophet, the Commander of the Faithful uses the adjective "honorable" to indicate that there was not weakness regarding this matter, i.e. the Prophet's father and moth (were both chaste and pious. Also, his birth was honorable in respect to circumstances of time and place.

Questions and Answers

Q. Can people, other than the Prophets establish connection with God through revelation? If so, can we conclude that after the end of prophethood too, God inspires His pure beings with some mysteries?

A. The answer to this question lies in the different between revelation and inspiration. Revelation is the descension of specific concepts together with their special wordings to a Prophet. The Holy Qur'an is, in the eyes of the Muslims, a revelation sent down to the Prophet of Islam through Gabriel. It is completely different from what ordinary human beings receive in their hearts or understands in an unusual manner.

Theirs are inspirations that pure, faithful and sincere creatures of God occasionally receive. Thus, revelation is far beyond inspiration and there is no matter if some people are inspired with some secrets in the period after the end o prophethood.

Q. If all the Prophets have had the same line and direction why have their followers, who have to practice their, commandments, not followed the same way?

A. The reason is that the followers of the Prophets were gradually deceived, that is, as time passed, malicious an(ignorant hands were put to work, beguiling the followers and distorting the teachings of the Prophets.

Q. What is, wilayat-al-faqih (the guardianship of religious jurisprudents)? Is it among the "Essentials of Religion" or among the "Secondary Principles" of Religion?

A. "Wilayat" means the guardianship of the community and faqih» is a jurisprudent or theologian. Thus, "wilayat- al-faqih" is the guardianship of the Islamic community by the religious theologians or jurisprudents in the period when the immaculate Imam is absent. It is one of the "Secondary Principles of Religion", a ruling system, and those who do not believe in it and deny it are disbelievers in Islam.

Q. What are common to monotheistic religions and what are their differences?

A. The doctrinal principles which they offer are common to all monotheistic religions (i.e. heavenly religions, for we do not have non-monotheistic heavenly religions), and the differences among them lie perhaps in the special decrees and commandments, each of them provides for that specific era in which it is founded.

Lesson Seven

Q. What is ijtihad?

A. Its literal meaning is «to try or endeavor» but in its technical sense it refers to a theologian's effort in understanding Islamic rules and regulations and deriving them from the Book (the Holy Qur'an), Traditions, etc. through the special skill he has acquired in his long course of discipleship under great Islamic experts and authorities. A person who has the ability to perform this job is called a «Mujtahid.».

Q. Why did the Prophet of Islam appear among the Arabs and not among the Persians, for example? Is it true that had he not appeared among the Arabs, the Arabian civilization would have been forgotten?

A. There is no definite reason concerning this matter but perhaps it can be argued that since Arabs were the most untrained and uneducated as well as the most quarrelsome nation of that time, and since they could more easily be affected and influenced than others, they possessed a proper background for the acceptance of the Prophet's invitation to Islam. Their lack of education and training was not, however, an obstacle to their acceptance of the invitation but, rather, caused more trouble and distress for the Prophet in attracting their attention.

Perhaps if this religion appeared among other nations, it would be more difficult to convince them. Arabs, though fastened to the chain of superstitions, possessed certain privileges such as bravery, devotion, tolerance (against hardship) and freedom (not being under the rule of satanic powers) which made them the most deserving nation to be exposed to this heavenly religion of Islam.

As to the Arabian civilization it should be said that the Arabs, having a civilization, a culture and a history of their own, would not have been forgotten, had the Prophet not appeared among them, in the same way as the Turks, Tajiks, Spaniards and so forth have remained up to this day.

Lesson Eight: The Believer' Status Before, After and at the Time of the Prophets' Appearance

In another sermon of the Nahjul Balaghah known as "al-Khutbah al-Qasi'ah" (*The Sermon of Disparagement*), the Commander of the Faithful lays down and explains some of the matters which were quoted in previous from Sermon No. 1, concerning the status of the people during the Age of Ignorance, conditions of the time of the appearance of the Prophets and the situation of the people after the appointment of the Prophets to prophethood.

He portrays, in effect, the conditions and circumstances, which had naturally cast shadows over the people's lives in the Age of Ignorance as well as the victorious status, the people gained after the appearance of the Prophets under the light of their efforts, struggles and endeavors.

Lessons from the Nahjul Balagha

A study of some of the statements of this Sermon (al-qasrah) which adds to our mind concerning what we learned about the background to prophethood, the Prophets' responsibilities, etc., in previous lessons, would bring us to a sound conclusion for this book. In a part of this Sermon we read: «think about the condition of people from among the believers who passed before you. What distress and trials[9] they underwent:»[10]

It means that we should look deep into the circumstances of the believers who lived before us, not treating them in a perfunctory manner because we cannot learn much from the formal appearance of the past events. Only when one traces the causes of these events and contemplates them deeply will one perceive that the believers of the past have been under severe pressure' and that they have been subjected to such hardships as hunger, torture, imprisonment and so

---

[9] In the terminology of the Qur'an and in Islamic usage "trial" (*bala*) comes to mean a bitter and a severe incident. Through these incidents, the human heroes have always been tried in the course of history and one cannot claim to be a perfect human being unless one exposes.

[10] Nahjul Balaghah of 'Ali, part two, page 410.

Lesson Eight

forth and greater hardships than those we suffer today, i.e. facing political problems and happenings and recognizing the true character of different groups and fronts and the stance they take.

The Commander of the Faithful continues with the following statements, "Were they the most over- burdened among all the people and in the most straightened circumstances in the whole world?"

The true believers have always been the most overburdened, the most pain suffering and the poorest creatures of God before the advent of the Prophets and the realization of Islamic revolutions (all the revolutions led by the Prophets have been Islamic in the sense that they have all been primarily aimed at submission to God). Why?

First, because the believers have to provide for their own sustenance. In fact, the true believers, those who have touched the spirit of the belief in God, never compromise with oppressive powers. They usually refuse to enter their service and to help them should they not be able to fight them."

Thus, under tyrannical governments, the believers are constantly face to face with hardships and inconveniences as far as their economic affairs are concerned. This can be traced in Islamic traditions. On the contrary, disbelievers compromise with the oppressors very easily, enter the service and thus enjoy a comfortable life.

Second, in addition to providing for their own living, the believers are usually obliged to shoulder the burden of the oppressors' impositions concerning their luxurious life. As an example, we all know that the overthrown regime (of Pahlavi) faced exorbitant expenses, which had to be paid by those who did not compromise with it. Those who compromised with that regime were not subjected to such burdens and impositions. They themselves took advantage of the prevailing situations as well.

Third, the believers have to tolerate the political impositions of the oppressive ruling powers with whom they fight. Such powers do not let them express their beliefs and have their own free thoughts and opinions. They force the believers to accept their own oppressive thoughts. Thus, the prevailing strangulation in a society is a great burden on the shoulder of the believers who refuse to adhere to the thoughts and opinions imposed by the oppressive ruling powers. They are, in effect, the most combative people, always fighting the oppressors in order to eradicate calamities and corruptions.

It is narrated that the believer is always in a state of struggling in some way or other. Under unlawful and corruptive governments, he involves himself in organized hidden and underground battles and lives in a precautionary, dissimulative manner, and under lawful, legitimate governments, he deals with political, ideological and military involvements or fights the enemy to safeguard the way of God. Thus, the believer is always in a fighting state, which is very troublesome. Fighting does not necessarily mean receiving wounds and bearing distress. It includes, in addition to these, fears and failures, worries and anxieties. The true fighter is thus the one who does not surrender to these and who only fights for the sake of God and duty, not for the sake of victory. Accordingly, fighting is more troublesome and difficult than all the trials of life.[11]

Finally the Commander of the Faithful says, that are the poorest and the most straightened people because they have to live in a state of strangulation, poverty, force and precautionary silence.

He continues to explain the believers' status in the following statements: "The Pharaohs took them as slaves. They inflicted the worst punishments and bitter sufferings on them. They continuously remained in this state of

---

[11] Akhavan-i-Thalith, one of the forerunners of modern Persian poetry, wrote a poem entitled "Wolves and Dogs" in which he pictures the status of rebellious believers with all hardships and calamities they suffer and their battle against oppressors as well as the status of the peace-seeking disbelievers and hypocrites who compromise with tyrants and do not refuse to he subjected to meanness. Akhvan likens the believers to wolves, which keep distance with the affluent and expose themselves to great sufferings for a loaf of bread, and compares the disbelievers with dogs, which always serve faithfully, collar on the neck, in order to receive what is left over the master's table.

Lesson Eight

(spiritual) ruinous disgrace and severe subjugation. They found no method for escape and no way for protection."

The first statement implies that the believers were forcefully made to obey Pharaohs (holders of tyrannical power) or deities other than the One God, although they were servants of God by nature. Sometimes, of course, such deities or objects of worship believe in God themselves and, therefore submission to them is submission to God. But when they induce people to the worship of their own selves, submission to them is submission to non-gods. It has been narrated he who listens to a speaker, becomes his servant. If the speaker speaks of God, that person will be the servant of God and if he speaks of Satan that person will be the servant of Satan.»

And Satan is sometimes the very human 'self' and 'concupiscence' to whose obedience the Pharaohs forced the believers in God, who knew no way of defending their human dignity and getting rid of such servitude.

Such was the status of the believers in God and followers of the Prophets who dealt with satanic ruling powers before the victory.

The Three-Act Play of People's Status

The status of the people before, during and after the Prophets' appointment can be likened to a three- act play, the first act of which shows hardship and distress, the second speaks of resistance and perseverance and the third pictures, victory and freedom. In fact, the believers will never gain victory without resisting hardships and struggling for their aim. The Commander of the Faithful continues, "Till when God, the Glorified, noticed that they were enduring troubles in His love and bearing distress and of fear for Him, He provided escape from the distress of trials. So, He changed their disgrace into honor and fear into safety."

In these statements, the Imam shows that the direction of the believers' struggles is towards God and they tolerate hardships and undesirable problems such as hunger, torture, imprisonment, cudgel- punishments and so

Lesson Eight

forth upon His way and for the sake of His love so that God, seeing their patience and perseverance, would reveal to them the ways of escape from nuisances and calamities, maintain their convenience and tranquility, change their disgrace into honor and fear into security and finally their defeat into victory.

It should be added here that honor (i.e. not submitting to contempt) and safety (i.e. not fearing any enemy) are the most important things the oppressed people are concerned about. Under the rule of satans (tyrannical powers) the people are not immune concerning their lives, properties, and morality and so forth, whereas under the rule of God and the oppressed people such worries and anxieties do not exist at all.

The Commander of the Faithful continues his discussion with these statements, "Consequently, they became ruling authorities and conspicuous leaders, and God's favors over them reached limits to which their own wishes had not reached," meaning that the whole community of believers, after God, bestowed victory upon them, became leaders (Imams, guides and patterns) and objects of imitation for other oppressed people and nations who followed their ways and manners and made movements.

This is clearly observable in the world of today in which a nation of believers (i.e. Iranians), after having struggled for a long time and gaining victory over a tyrannical regime, has now become the leader of the whole world of the oppressed, and achievement which had never been imagined by Iranians.

They thought, in fact, about victory but they never imagined to become leaders and guiding patterns for all of the oppressed people of the world such as those of Saudi Arabia, Iraq, Egypt, Persian Gulf countries, Africa and America, who have been greatly influenced and motivated by Iranians' achievements. And this is nothing but God's favor as he says.

Lesson Eight

Conclusion: Two General Points in the Sermon

First, in this Sermon (No. 191) the emphasis is mostly on the spiritual aspects of the people's calamities and adversities.. In fact, such factors as strangulation, lack of security, the burden of mental impositions and the burden of providing for the satanic wishes of illegitimate governments, all of which cause humanity to suffer spiritually and invoke one to campaign, are more emphasized than such material misfortunes (or trials) as hunger for which the people rarely campaign. To say the least, human beings' honor and dignity are the dearest things to them, which stimulate them to seriously struggle and campaign. Hunger and the like can be removed in other ways. These are the points of emphasis in this Sermon.

Secondly, the Imam emphasizes here that in a community of believers, when the arrogant government is overthrown, it is the oppressed that take it over another arrogant group. As an example, after the revolution of Moses and destruction of Pharaoh, it was the believers themselves and the masses that became rulers and established a true government.

Also, during the lifetime of the Last Prophet, as well as during the reign of the rightly guided Caliphs, the people themselves were masters of their own affairs and played significant roles in resolving the matters which came about. They loved the Prophet and accepted what he said but not blindly and under propagandic pressures. They freely accepted his decisions and they themselves made minor decisions.

Unfortunately, as time has passed, people's participation in and contribution to the ruling affairs of the Islamic communities have gradually decreased and these communities have turned out to be, like the communities predominated by ignorance, consisting of two classes of people - the arrogant and the deprived; whereas a true Islamic community consists only of one class of people and they are the believers.

www.ingramcontent.com/pod-product-compliance
Lightning Source LLC
Chambersburg PA
CBHW021445070526
44577CB00002B/263